599.757096 F943
Frump, Robert.
The man-eaters of Eden

D0966802

THE MAN-EATERS OF EDEN

THE MAN-EATERS OF EDEN

Life and Death in Kruger National Park

ROBERT R. FRUMP

THE LYONS PRESS
GUILFORD, CONNECTICUT
AN IMPRINT OF THE GLOBE PEQUOT PRESS

599.757096
F943

To buy books in quantity for corporate use
or incentives, call **(800) 962–0973, ext. 4551,**
or e-mail **premiums@GlobePequot.com.**

Copyright © 2006 by Robert R. Frump

ALL RIGHTS RESERVED. No part of this book may be reproduced or transmitted in any form by any means, electronic or mechanical, including photocopying and recording, or by any information storage and retrieval system, except as may be expressly permitted in writing from the publisher. Requests for permission should be addressed to The Lyons Press, Attn: Rights and Permissions Department, P.O. Box 480, Guilford, CT 06437.

The Lyons Press is an imprint of The Globe Pequot Press.

10 9 8 7 6 5 4 3 2 1

Printed in the United States of America

Designed by Carol Sawyer/Rose Design

ISBN-13: 978-1-59228-892-2
ISBN-10: 1-59228-892-8

Library of Congress Cataloging-in-Publication Data is available on file.

KENT FREE LIBRARY

For Tom Masland

Rex libertatis sum

8/10/06.   24.95

For obvious reasons conservationists often deny that large predatory animals actually kill people, but there is ample evidence that such indignant denial is nonsense.

—Hans Kruuk, honorary professor of zoology at the University of Aberdeen, Scotland

CONTENTS

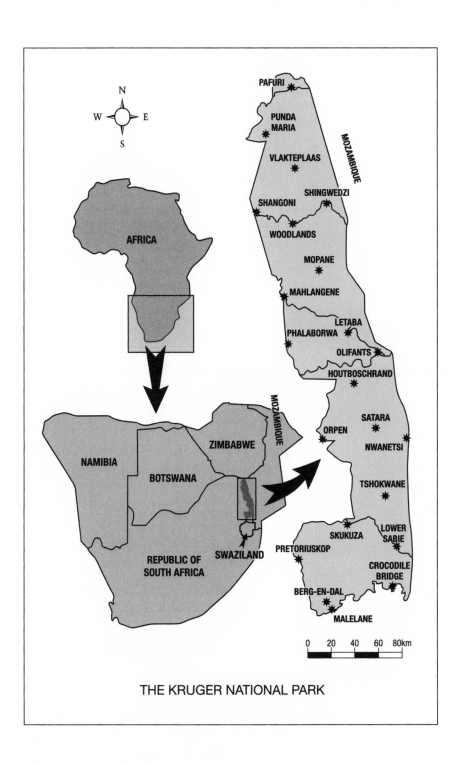

THE KRUGER NATIONAL PARK

PREFACE

This book is written as a work of narrative nonfiction. It tells a story. I prefer a narrative approach to nonfiction because the telling of a story presents facts in an accessible manner within a context of nuance and emotion. Observations, conclusions, interpretations, nuance, and opinion in this form of writing belong to the narrator-writer and fairly so, I feel, if that disclosure between writer and reader is fully made.

This does not give the writer license to mint fact and I've attempted to address concerns about fact here through the inclusion of endnotes to any statement that is not attributed in the text outright. Endnotes alone are no antidote to the misuse of facts or their use out of context, but it is my hope they send a signal of purpose: I do not take facts lightly. Nor do I knowingly misrepresent them. As the late Patrick Moynihan once said, "Everyone is entitled to his own opinion, but not his own facts."[1] You will find opinion and interpretation here, but the facts are, well, the facts.

So there are no "compound characters" here, no hypothetical scenes presented as real. This story is not "fact based" or "inspired by true events." To the best of my ability, I've written a story that I believe presents the facts of the situation and, with luck, some truths as well.

Note: the summary before each chapter is representative of late-nineteenth- and early-twentieth-century nonfiction accounts of explorations.

Robert R. Frump
January 14, 2006
Summit, New Jersey

PROLOGUE

For more than a year now, I've studied lions and man-eaters, and I feel I should know better, behave better, be braver.

But when I hear the sound in the predawn hours, as I walk alone over land as flat and long as a parade ground in the ink-black dark of an African night, something far older than intellect plays out.

Basso profundo, rumbling in from the bushveld, so low it is nearly subsonic, not near, but not far either, comes the roar of male lions. Once, twice, four times in all, a pause, and then again, leisurely, measured, dominant, with all the time in the world, fully held whole notes: five more low, slow roars.

The wave of sound reverberates first in my breastbone, then locks up some part of my brain and freezes me midstep like a lizard caught in the open on a flat rock.

I am not frightened—just frozen. I've no clear idea how that happened. Only later do I put my finger on it, in a sentence buried midway through a book about prey species' behavior.[2] The freeze behavior is part of a defense mechanism known broadly as "crypsis." Freezing instantly is an automatic antipredatory measure hardwired into our systems. A part of the brain called the amygdala contains unconscious memories and fears of predators that threatened our ancestors. The threats in modern times mostly are gone. The amygdala could not care less. Let an unexpected sight or sound of a predator pop up, and the amygdala grabs control before conscious thought occurs.

So the lions' roars triggered my amygdala, and the amygdala froze me midstep. Motion means detection. Detection could mean death. Useful in ancient times, no doubt, but now, after a moment more, I reassure myself that it is stupid to be worried. I'm inside a high, barbed-wire confinement in the heart of Kruger National Park in South Africa.

I don't move, though, for in an instant that comforting thought is overwhelmed by darker thoughts that I've done my research too well. The workers eaten at Tsavo in Kenya long ago were inside thorn bomas—arguably a harder target than these barbed wire fences.[3] The people killed in Tanganyika—more than one thousand of them six decades ago—often were inside hard mud huts with thatched roofs, which the lions shucked like so many pistachio shells.[4] The wife of the head of Kruger security was killed inside a barricaded camp larger than this one only two years before my visit.[5] And the park acknowledges that many of the Kruger lions, if not outright man-eaters, certainly have eaten humans.[6]

These are not good thoughts. Not for what I have planned at least. I stay frozen in midstride, one foot forward, one foot back, both feet on the ground. Two hundred yards away light plays from a lamppost where I am supposed to meet two Kruger rangers for a dawn foot patrol. As I measure the distance to the light, my eyes are drawn to the nearest trees.

Scientists have charted what can happen to my amygdala and me if things do not improve and my systems do not "stand down." My pupils will dilate, to give me a better chance of detecting predators. The bronchioles in my lungs will dilate, too, all the better for flight or fight. Blood pressure and pulse will pump up as well. All these things may already have happened, in fact.

Then, in my liver, glycogen will break down, providing a quick source of energy. Adrenaline will flood my bloodstream, and my spleen will contract in order to send out more white blood cells in case they are needed to repel infection. The capillaries in my stomach and intestines will contract as well, sending blood to my muscles.

Then things will get even stranger. My body will prepare the bladder and the colon for evacuation. And my body hair may stand on end. "Piloerection" it is called. Some think this is a display mechanism intended to make the "prey" (me) look larger.[7] Somewhere in there, a basic decision will be made, often not determined by thought. Flee? Or stand and fight?

And if actually caught by a lion? With luck, from what I have read, endorphins will flood my system, giving me a sort of distanced and not unpleasant dreamlike view of my plight. They will anesthetize me near totally from pain.[8] Then again, they may not. Some survivors of lion attacks say the endorphins never kicked in.[9] They suffered severe pain. Endorphin doping seems to vary from person to person.

I remain frozen for a moment more, hear the roars again, and realize the lions are heading away from the gates of Satara, the large tourist enclosure known as "the cat camp" in Kruger. I chuckle at my inner lizard, take a deep breath, regain my composure, then resume the walk to the ranger rendezvous point.

But for a full minute or two, I knew a little of what it is like for the Mozambican refugees who walk through this park at night. They were out there then, almost certainly. They heard the same roars. They had the same reaction I did. And some of them might have all the other reactions too, including the reactions to attacks.

Unlike me, they have no rangers, no lights, no barbed-wire protection. Only the trees or fire. Even then, fire and a tree did little for those four back in 1997 up north near Punda Maria. The Punda pride took them down one at a time, one at the fire, three from the tree. Only the one refugee bobbing about in the thin upper branches survived.[10]

It is way too dark. So are these thoughts. I walk a little faster. A lot faster. But I do not run. You should never run. At the very least, I remember that much. Of all that I have read and seen of man-eaters, I remember that and carefully slow my gait.

Still, my amygdala and I are moving at a pretty good clip.

Robert R. Frump
Satara Camp
Kruger National Park, South Africa
4:45 A.M.
Tuesday, August 6, 2002

THE MAN-EATERS OF EDEN

Chapter 1

THE AUNT IN THE ATTIC

A casual wave from the bush; a terrible discovery; a ranger takes an oath; questions arise and an investigative safari is organized and begun.

My journey started with a story and a question. Neville Edwards first told me the story and asked his question in this manner.

He was guiding two Frenchmen through the very heart of lion country in South Africa's wild Kruger National Park when a hand rose up from the bush and waved a casual good morning hello.

At the same time, a magnificent elephant bull ambled across the grand vista that was Kruger. Neville's clients—two very senior corporate VIPs out to admire their fellow carnivores—did not see the hand. They were pointing up front at the big tusker and talking excitedly. Always, with elephants, you kept a sharp eye and you kept the Land Rover in reverse, ready to go in case of a charge. That and all the other rules of the bush, Neville Edwards understood well, for he was a veteran safari guide with years of experience.

But this hand? This wave? Edwards did not understand it and he could not ignore it. No one should be in the wild of Kruger on foot, but now the hand was summoning him. With an odd tremble, it seemed to gesture him forward, beckoning.

He brought his binoculars to the spot to see what the person wanted, focused the murky oval field of his vision, and it was then

1

that the black-backed jackal popped crisply into view. The scavenger was worrying an arm of the dead body it was attached to. The hand danced above, still waving. Then the jackal changed its grip. The hand and arm dropped and a human head flopped into view and fell, flopped and fell, impossibly relaxed.

There was a brief moment for Edwards when lucid thoughts crossed his mind. A woman's hand, he thought, not a man's, as the fingers were slender. A Mozambique refugee, he knew. The poor woman! She had tried it—tried to walk the Kruger. Dead but not long dead, he thought; she was still flexible. The lions that had killed her were not far away now; they must just have let the jackal in to clean up.

Then Edwards lost it. The jackal began gulping, as jackals do, gorging all it could in case the lions returned. At the sight, a shiver from the base of Edward's spine tingled up to the top of his scalp and demanded that most basic choice of action: fight or flight?

No choice really. Kruger guides traveled unarmed and the lions were still near. So flight was imperative, away from the lions, yes, but also from the body and a concept where humans were prey and protein and the food chain had been inverted.

Neville fumbled for the radio and keyed the mike. He started to yell to base camp in English, "I need help!"—then thought better of it, in case the Frenchmen might understand. They had not seen and they did not need to. It was Bastille Day after all, and Edwards ever was considerate. He switched to Zulu: "Ifuna siza! Ifuna siza!"

Then, to the amazement and protest of the French tourists, Edwards floored the Landie away from the only game they would see that day. He accelerated, away from the elephant, away from the jackal, and most particularly away from the woman and the horror she stood for: humans as prey and protein. Edwards just did not care. The VIPs were no longer the alpha predators in that part of the world. Nor was he. Nor the poor woman.

Later that day, July 14, 2000, he poured a strong drink, knocked it back, and swore an oath, "No more safaris! Ever!" And he asked himself the question he could not answer: how could all this have occurred in Kruger, billed always in the books and posters as "the Eden of Africa?"[11]

In truth, at some level of consciousness, all the players behind the curtain at Eden, even those who had not seen the bloody proof smacked down whole on the table, had been asking that question for some time. The rangers, the safari guides, the field biologists, and the conservation managers of the great park—"the Kruger," as they almost all call it in awe and respect—knew the stories about the lions and the refugees. Bits of bloody clothes found in the middle of nowhere. A lone suitcase, filled, abandoned in the bush. A single shoe. A full water bottle. Footprints that trekked on, then just ended. Everyone knew what was happening. Kruger was the one best way for poor Mozambicans to enter South Africa with its supply of jobs and relative safety. Kruger presented the longest South African border with Mozambique and the cover the Mozambicans needed to sneak in. Kruger also had more than two thousand lions, few with any reason to fear humans.

Edwards was the last professional ranger and guide I talked to at the end of a tourist safari in South Africa, and his job technically was "transfer"—getting my family and me safely to the airport to return to the States. The previous days had been spent in the bush—if you could call the "bush" luxury safari camps with showers, hot tubs, and gourmet meals, and with well-educated, literate young rangers who could answer virtually any question about the wild of Africa. I was not looking for a "story." In fact, I was on holiday in March 2001, looking for a break and a visit with Tom Masland and his family. He had been the best man at our wedding many years ago, and was then *Newsweek*'s correspondent in sub-Saharan Africa. He knew his way around the continent the way I know the block where I live.

It was a great break. The rangers and their sidekick trackers struck me as the best of men and women—intelligent and attuned both to the wilderness and what they themselves loved. I consider myself an ardent conservationist, a green-leaning lover of the outdoors, an amateur who knows a modest bit of flora and fauna. I grew up in farm country in the Midwest, where you hunt your first pheasant at age ten. A while back, for a magazine article, I spent a week in the wild learning how to track. I can start a fire pretty easily without matches. In a casual, unplanned, and often clumsy manner over the years, I've backpacked through rain forests and up mountain switchbacks, kayaked through riptides and surf, set foot on glaciers, been dropped near remote lakes by bush pilots, camped in the deep snow, hiked remote wilderness beaches, built shelters from branches and leaves, canoed through remote lands, been dumped into Class IV waters, and heard howling wolves close by in the wilderness.

In short, I knew enough to know that here I knew very little. The rangers and trackers had skills far, far beyond mine. They could see sign and tracks in the subtlest variations of undergrowth and bent twigs. One literally tracked a leopard over rock—a feat I thought impossible until I saw the tracks emerge into mud on the far side of the rock formation. The tracker, a Shangan, found the leopard four hours later. We would have been as happy had we just watched the tracker at work. What was invisible to me popped out in bas-relief to him. So it is when you have done something for many years with great interest and passion.

The less admirable aspect of being a ranger or tracker revealed itself slowly. On that first trip to South Africa, in the private reserves, we would drive within feet of lions in the daytime, and the animals would seem indifferent to our presence, if they noted us at all. Rangers on these private reserves outside Kruger were asked whether lions ever attacked humans, and they would answer something like, "Never here. Never here while you're in the vehicle." Then some of them would pause and add, "Not here. But *Kruger*? Not tourists but with refugees? That's another story."[12]

And if you were to meet a new ranger, skip the preliminaries, and ask him flat out about Kruger, he would almost inevitably show two reactions in quick succession. First, a look of keen interest and engagement would cross his face, the look of the field biologist and earnest explorer of nature that he was. Then would come a suspicious and hurt look and the question, "Who told you about Kruger?" This, inevitably, was the look of someone in the tourist trade, I thought, someone who was vaguely threatened. Afraid that "it" would get out. Afraid that it already had.

The private guides avoided my questions so frequently that every evasion stoked my curiosity, of course. Then, on the last day of the trip, as it turned out, I met Neville Edwards, who seemed afraid of little, save perhaps that summons from the waving hand under the acacia tree on a stretch of Kruger lowveld.

The hand beckoned to me as well. My jumble of thoughts took form around that story and the other clusters of conversations, ordered themselves, and then marched me off on a trip without my really knowing it at the time. Neville's story, on top of the beginnings of so many others, was the catalyst. It was the last piece, the last co-incidence that convinced me that I might spend some weeks in search of facts and truths in the bush of Kruger and months more in books and papers about the lions of Kruger and the refugees of Mozambique and the crossed paths the two species traveled.

My wife saw it too. "We should follow up on this," Suzanne said, and I nodded in a sort of noncommittal way as Neville drove us to the airport. But already I was planning the return trip as we were ending the first.

The project of an investigative safari seemed on balance worthwhile and its end product more than pulp nonfiction. The first of all classic plots of all stories is "Overcoming the Monster." Literary critic Christopher Booker, among others, tells us that in his book *The Seven Basic Plots*.[13] So the story claimed pedigree. Moreover, most all stories tell us something about our spot on the evolutionary ladder. This one was just more literal.

Above all, when it turns out that we are being eaten regularly in great numbers by large predators, an examination of such a situation could be considered instructional to the species. Oxford historian Felipe Fernandez-Armesto seems to have reasoned in somewhat the same manner. In his book *Millennium: A History of the Last Thousand Years* two of the seven-hundred-plus pages in his book deal with the famous man-eating lions of Tsavo in 1898.[14] The disproportionate significance of Tsavo and the significance of Kruger are the same. They posed threshold questions of civilization and "progress." We may have not solved all problems and plagues, but lions are not *supposed* to eat people in man's modern natural order of things. Yet lions were, at Tsavo and in Kruger, too, more than one hundred years later.

How could that have happened? And what did humans do about it? What did they *not* do?

My thought was to examine the Kruger situation dispassionately, without the hysteria of an "exposé." The basic facts were broadly known, so in that sense there was no exposé. The rangers and the park officials acknowledged the problem, but treated the phenomenon as they might a mad aunt in the attic. Everyone knew. They all heard the mad thumping upstairs. But no one in the parlor addressed the situation in polite company.

Certainly no one would say how many had been killed, and it was clear no count has been kept. Record books on this subject should have been closed, I had thought, a hundred years ago. The Tsavo man-eaters were among the most famous. Some counts say they claimed more than one hundred before the famous British hunter and engineer John H. Patterson finally shot them. But those were in the days of pith helmets and the Empire—the late nineteenth century.[15]

True, in Tanganyika, from 1932 through 1947, lions had killed and eaten about fifteen hundred humans—considered the "All-Africa record,"[16] as one writer put it—before famous white hunter George Rushby dispatched them. But that occurred in the confusion of a global war, when one could argue that civilization had, well, slipped a tad.

How big was the Kruger kill? No one hazarded a guess even unofficially, though most agreed it long ago had passed measurement by the dozen. It seemed likely to me that given the broad acceptance of the problem and the fact that little was being done to solve it, we might well have a new All-Africa on our hands, a record the park officials and South African government were falling over themselves *not* to claim.

And so it seemed a simple and straightforward story, and in the modern world, with its assumption of progress and absolute values, it would have been just that.

But in the postmodern world—Po-Mo World, an artist friend calls it—the one certainty is that absolutes refract to irony. The simple truths I sought soon prismed into gothic complexities and a nuanced noir that Colonel Patterson, Rushby, Peter Capstick, Robert Ruark, Jim Corbett, and the other great white hunters and adventure writers of past centuries might never have foreseen.

The orbits of monster and hero—of Grendel and Beowulf—had altered. The archetypes of Western culture—laid forth in the epic poem *Beowulf* dating from before 1000 AD—were present. But Grendel the monster and Beowulf the hero circled each other in a profoundly different ellipse. They seemed somehow to have swapped polar charges.

There was a new type of victim, a new type of hero, and a new type of monster. In the postmodern world, the victims—the Mozambicans—had few friends and seemed to be portrayed as more villain than victim. Grendel—the lions of Kruger—was seen by most as holding the moral, high, green ground. At an extreme, some went so far as to say a breed of man-eaters helped provide security and very effective immigration control agents.

And the modern Beowulfs—the rangers—were conflicted at best. It was a bad time to play hero on this postmodern stage. Slay the monster and you got booed. Let it pass and you felt guilty. The rangers, the men and women I had come to know and respect, were caught in an existential puzzle where there were extra pieces. Carefully over the years, they had pieced Kruger together as one of the world's great parks. But *this* part of it? Lions eating humans consistently for years and years? They genuinely and quite earnestly could not figure where those pieces fit in the tableau of Eden. Over the years, they had accomplished a great unquestionable good that had resulted in this one unintended consequence.

So those were the facts and hidden truths I saw at play in the park. And as for me, well, I may have styled myself as the remote and inquiring observer of these matters, and that truly was my intent. I intended no harm to the lions and thought Kruger and the lions should last forever. My youthful hunting days were for the most part long, long gone. Lions in Kruger as elsewhere still faced incredible pressures from poaching, cruel snares, and so-called canned hunts. In recent years, outbreaks of bovine tuberculosis have infected lions, and the disease has been taking a terrible toll. Some scientists estimated that the wild lion population was only twenty thousand in all of Africa—down from some two hundred thousand in the 1980s.[17] I felt their preservation was absolutely vital.

As for the refugees, I wished them safe passage or a long-awaited peace and prosperity in their homeland. In the same way that poor Mexicans inevitably are drawn north across the U.S. border, so were the Mozambicans drawn west through Kruger. It was inevitable, an economic osmosis. Strict border controls always work poorly if there is a strong black-market demand from a neighboring country. Or a disaster in yours. Many sought jobs in South Africa. Many others were trying to stave off starvation and for many years the genocidal campaigns of a seemingly endless civil war. So long had Mozambique been at war that an AK-47 was a prominent feature of its flag even in peacetime. Of course, all countries need border controls. But whatever the crimes of the Mozambicans, being eaten in Eden was a far too cruel, but not unusual, punishment.

So it seemed to me I would be on a balanced path. Even from the start, though, I knew there were journalistic and stylistic land mines on that path, and I would almost certainly step on a few.

Writing that involves science and carnivores splits into many camps. Scientists and science writers often decry attention to the emotions and drama of humans coming into contact with animals that want to eat them. One science writer I admire characterized the reports about Tsavo written by Colonel Patterson as "predator pornography."[18] Two scientist authors of a superb book, *Man the Hunted*, suggested that a front-page story in the *New York Times* about wolves eating villagers in India was sensationalist when 300 million people in that country were malnourished, a story rarely told.[19]

The science writers and scientists have a point. But they also miss a few small points and one very big one. The small points include their miscalculation of "sensationalist" authors. Judging Colonel Patterson's early nineteenth-century conclusions by twenty-first-century standards of knowledge simply is not fair. As for the *New York Times*, it can be faulted for many things but its famine coverage is not among them. Besides, both Patterson and the *Times* on their most sensational day pale in comparison to the lavishly purpled but finely wrought prose of author Peter Capstick. ("Coming up, he shouted and yelled at the lion to draw its attention and then blew the cat's head into pudding with his own .458.")[20]

The larger mistake scientists can make is to ignore the emotional dimension of large carnivores eating humans, the drama that Patterson and Capstick capture. Perhaps this is because the scientists cannot measure the emotion. Nevertheless, it may well be the drama, the adrenaline, the fear of failure, the courage and triumph that shape the relationship of our two species and always have. Capstick may indeed write, well, vividly some days ("The man-eater gave a terrific tug and the claws ripped forward tearing De Beer's scalp loose from his skull until it hung over his face like a dripping, hairy, red beret.").[21] But there is a reason why such passages are of interest to us and why scientists should avoid dismissing that interest merely as a titillating response to "predator porn."

Hans Kruuk, a professor of zoology respected worldwide and author of *Hunter and Hunted*, weighs in on this point in explaining the approach he takes in his book. "The stories are bloody, and some readers may be put off by the gory detail. Such a reaction is part of our anti-predator behavior. But I think that the pattern of predation is important, as is how common the incidents are, because this is what makes up the threat which, in evolution, has shaped our response to predators."[22]

In this view, understanding the drama of predation is not just necessary. It may be definitive. Animals do not evolve because they do double-blind tests, regression analysis, and Monte Carlo simulations to assess probabilities of outcome. Humans may inject some reason into the process of change, but oftentimes human behavior is glandular, emotional, drama-charged, caused by "risk-relevant stimuli."

I am closer to the Kruuk than the Capstick school in such matters, but discount neither. So it should be noted that some of the stories here are bloody and emotional because some of the human contact with predators is bloody and emotional. In fact, it seems to me that without the emotional involvement and the drama of human and predator behavior there would not be places like Kruger, and lions would be mounted museum exhibits, not living in the Eden of Kruger.

The complexity of the minefield I faced did not end with questions of literary style and the relevance of emotions, however. Conservationists themselves divide into at least two camps. There are those who think nature is best preserved when it has some economic use. In this view, hunting of old lions, say, may be permissible. The lions would die soon anyway and if a few Western sportsmen want to pay $50,000 to ethically and fairly pursue and shoot the animals, then that gives jobs to the local citizens and helps protect lions. It gives the lion an economic reason for existing. One reason numbers of lions have declined so drastically, say the economic theorists, is that lion hunting has been banned in many countries, thus removing the economic incentive of keeping lions alive.

The converse view is that nature and rare species should be preserved because it is the right thing to do whether that preservation serves an economic purpose or not. John Muir, the well-known American conservationist, is among the most famous of those holding this view. He split with friends who thought wilderness should be managed "for the betterment of mankind" and became known as a "preservationist." Some land, preservationists feel, is sacred ground and needs to be treated with that respect. At an extreme? Hunting is not just killing; it is murder. That point seems less extremist in South Africa because of one very damaging point: a lot of the "hunts" these days are just "shoots"—the notorious "canned hunts" where the quarry never has a chance.

Some sort of brand would be applied to me for certain, I knew, because much of what I would find in my travels seemed to subvert the dominant paradigm of the green public, both schools of conservation, and many zoologists and field biologists. Thomas Kuhn, a physicist turned philosopher, popularized the word "paradigm" in the 1950s and 1960s in his examination of how scientific advances occurred.[23] He explained what happens when the scientific community is faced with a new paradigm that challenges the old paradigm, or when the old paradigm fails to solve a particularly important puzzle. The scientists turn a bit cranky and spend large amounts of energy attempting to fit the round pegs of new problems into the square holes of the old paradigm.

It may be a stretch to say I was suggesting a full paradigm shift in the sense Kuhn meant it. "Paradigm shift" these days is included in every third overcooked corporate PowerPoint presentation. But of some great change brewing in the way we viewed predators and conservation, there seemed no doubt. Kruuk's book, for example, challenges a sacred pillar of the current popular greenness—the assumption that the preservation of large predators is universally a good thing. Kruuk takes on that one about as directly as possible when he notes, "For obvious reasons conservationists often deny that large animals actually kill people, but there is ample evidence that such indignant denial is nonsense."[24]

These were the things I was finding as well, and inevitably there would be some confrontations and controversy and at some point I risked being described as "anticonservation" or "anti-lion" or deconstructed as simply "unscientific." The ultimate questions I intended to ask were simple, the issues complex. Was a human life always more valuable than a lion's? If so, why was that not apparent in Kruger? And if it was *not* true, then what formulas and emotions were employed to calculate and determine the tipping point? When was it OK for humans to be killed by lions and the lions to live? Was the matter even under public—or scientific—discussion?

Those issues, I knew, could well be drowned out by emotional reactions of the various camps. In my worst dreams, the NRA, PETA, the Sierra Club, Savannas Forever, Greenpeace, Bono, Beowulf scholars, and Nelson Mandela himself all found common ground in condemning me.

So of those unavoidable intellectual dangers, I was certain from the start. Yet, there were times when I seemed to be creating dangers wholly of my own making. I developed some hidden plans that I kept from family, friends, and my guides, too. I came to believe that if I was to do the story right and capture the emotional element of it all, then somehow I needed to walk the park at night just as the Mozambicans did and experience what it was like to be prey.

It was a thought that came and went, but one that at times burned with such a clear flame that it seemed to me as if nothing short of crossing the park would let me keep the simplest and most basic tenet of a journalist's code: bear witness.

But there were many other codes at play as well in Kruger that I knew little of at the start. I would learn slowly and imperfectly that my plan to experience the refugees' plight firsthand would trigger ethical complexities as intricate as those faced by the rangers.

In that there is nothing new. The reasoned strategies and good intentions of naive Westerners carrying visions of Norse legends into the bush are upended every day in Africa. Then those strategies can be bowled back in an altered form to perplex the Westerner further.

Or so it seemed to me, looking back at it all later. My plan to experience what it felt like to be prey would fail miserably and make me feel more than a little sleazy for suggesting a night trek through Kruger. Then, without any plan at all, I would witness it in a manner different from any I would have conceived, in a situation that placed me a good bit closer to a lion at night than ever I care to be.

Of all those assorted things—the changed relationship of lion and human, my own quiet caldron of bubbling compulsion—I knew little as I started. It all seemed a straightforward story, the oldest story in the world: humans versus monsters. Retell and update the story of Grendel and Beowulf.

Naturally, there would be subtleties in the modern version. Humans would not literally wipe out all the lions. They would adjust systems, alter immigration laws, save the lions and the refugees. I was certain of it. Someone had to have a plan. This was postapartheid South Africa, the land of Mandela, of truth and reconciliation. I'd find the modern version of the armored Beowulf who slays the Man-Eating Beast—by fixing the system. In a world of complexity, this would be simple. My investigative safari would follow a clear path. I would learn about the rangers, the history of the park and the lions, the refugees and how they interacted, and then explain the situation, all in orderly fashion.

And so it was in July 2002 that my airplane came to touch down on the airfield just west of Kruger Park, and as they say in the old exploration books, with glad heart I began my journey in earnest.

Chapter 2

THE RANGERS

The park is revealed; two modern rangers and their childhood in the bush; deaths in the park; trial by croc; we encounter a leopard; a surprising revelation by a professional hunter.

Neville Edwards, Suzanne, and I rendezvoused near Kruger National Park and plotted the route of our journey through lion country.

He was the spotter and tracker on this trip, and his boyhood friend and proprietor of Esseness Safaris, Steve Gibson, was at the wheel. They would be my guides on this investigative safari, intent on finding answers to questions we've formulated after wading through a small library of books and papers about Kruger, rangers, lions, and man-eaters. Suzanne would be shooting photographs for a *Men's Journal* article.

My thought is to take the topics in neat order, and then order the book in the same manner. We would explore the history of the park and its rangers, understand the refugees' plight, examine the lions, describe how the two species interacted, and find an answer to the problem. Neither Neville nor Steve is employed by Kruger. They are freelance rangers and guides who contract with individuals or safari companies to show travelers the park or other wild areas of Africa, and they are knowledgeable but neutral about what Neville later would dub "lion politics."   .

For Edwards, the old vow—"No more safaris. Ever!"—lasted about a day. Safari guides in Africa, like fishing guides in the States, resign almost as regularly as they re-up. Now the great Kruger—a park about the size and shape of Massachusetts elongated and standing on end, three hundred miles from top to bottom, fifty miles wide—rolled out once again before Edwards. He was again a guide, a ranger, and I was a journalist with a story. Both of us were energized and glad to begin the safari on that July day in the winter of South Africa with its sunny days and its nights as crisp and cool as autumn in New Hampshire.

These are neither the flat plains of the Serengeti we are traveling nor stereotyped Hollywood jungle country. We are in the far northeast corner of South Africa, hard against the Mozambican border, with Zimbabwe straight north of us. For miles, rolling hills and scrubland roll on with yellow and brown thatching grass the exact coloring of a lion. Through this land, Mozambicans have migrated to South Africa for more than a century. They walk through Kruger because the great park comprises virtually the whole border of the two countries, and because the wildness of the park provides great cover from detection.

We are following the road near the Crocodile River—the southernmost route of the migrants—and with a regularity that suggests Spielbergian cues, giraffes hobbyhorse by. Then elephants heft and lever their great bulk across the grassland. Then zebras, then kudu, and whole shy herds of model-thin, lithe impalas, on invisible runways, all move warily at a walk, one foot squarely in front of the other, through the swaying, lion-colored grass. This grass is everywhere.

Superimposed upon these idyllic scenes is modernity. The roads are open to tourists. BMWs, VW microbuses, Audis, Mercedes, Volvos, Land Rovers, Nissans, and Toyotas; in singles, pairs, and sometimes packs, come, go, and stop, filled with tourists. Motor drives whir. Cars drive on. More cars stop. Video cams hum. These are the regular rhythms of Kruger, and it seems for the most part deceptively safe.

The lions, when we see them much later in daytime, are no threat. They morph up from the thatching grass and seem to be of the grass. They are a trick of the grass, an alchemy. A face forms from the light brown base metal. The head of a lioness, big black ears turned to us and tuned, looks out. The head then melts back to its base, disappears, then reforms a moment later at another angle. Later still, the grasses converge and bulge up into the much larger, square-jawed, maned-head of a male lion. The head turns to us in supreme boredom, then puddles back into its constituent element.

A moment later still, the male lion bounds languidly up from the grass and presents his full form. He moves. The lioness takes form and moves, too, but more slowly. He catches her. Foreplay is a growl, answered by a snarl. They mate. Seconds later, they separate. They amble. They mate again. Then puddle into the grass once more.

This is what can be seen from a car window on a normal day in Kruger, and scenes like this draw more than one million visitors a year and tens of millions of dollars and Euros to South Africa. White South Africans, particularly Afrikaners, feel a strong sense of heritage and history in the park, and they crowd the park on holiday. Yet so large is Kruger and so authentically wild that the visitors seem never to damp its sense of wildness and authenticity. Roughly 11,000 elephants, 150,000 impalas, 5,500 giraffes, 21,000 zebras, 20,000 buffalo, 1,500 warthogs, 2,500 white rhinos, 300 black rhinos, 10,000 wildebeests, 350 African wild dogs, 300 cheetahs, 2,000 hyenas, and 2,000 lions assure wildlife sightings.[25]

There is no, or little, danger to the tourists. Mostly the tourists are ignored and the cars have surprisingly little impact on the wildlife of the park. Cars and Land Rovers, big, hard-shelled objects with a foul smell and no known protein value, do not seem to bother the lions, and one can, given the right circumstances, quite commonly approach within feet. Edwards has seen a lioness lie in the shadow of his Land Rover, even jump to the hood and rest her head on his windshield for a nice snooze.

There is no danger to the tourists, or little of it. But this does not mean all is safe or that lions are the only threat. A young Kruger staff ranger was killed only four years ago when he stopped his night safari for a break. He walked ahead of the group of tourists and sat on a bridge railing, rifle in his lap. A leopard came from under the bridge and took him from behind. He died instantly, his rifle clattering on the bridge decking. The tourists had trouble driving the injured and starving animal away from the body.[26]

A year earlier, in the heart of "civilized Kruger," a woman park ranger—the wife of Kruger's security chief—was jogging alone within the protected enclave of the Skukuza rest camp, the ranger head-quarters of all of Kruger. A leopard ambushed her twenty yards from her home and killed her. A child of a Kruger employee met a similar fate in 2002, and in that same year a leopard stalked and attacked a ranger chopping firewood. The leopard sprang, the ranger swung. The man lived to tell the tale, amazed that such an ancient weapon as an ax and more ancient instincts saved him and killed the leopard. In 2003, another ranger was attacked by a leopard. He shot and killed the animal, but only after it had mauled his arm.[27]

Nor are big cats the only danger. As ranger Jan Roderigues once chronicled, the thin veneer of civilization can relax even seasoned rangers. They forget Eden is wild. Sometimes they are lulled and quite literally wade into trouble as several of them discovered in 1976. On a sunny Sunday summer day in November, Thomas Van Rooyen Ryssel and a good friend, Louis Olivier, joined some ranger colleagues and their families for a picnic along the Sabi River near the Skukuza rest camp.[28]

The Sabi ran shallow and nearly crystal clear here. The picnic was on the bank of the river, but Thomas and Louis and some others waded across to a small island. They thought nothing of it; the water did not even reach their knees. The rangers on the island talked, fished, joked, smoked, and laughed for a spell and then set out to return.

Frans Loubser, a park engineer, was leading the way, but as chance would have it, he turned back just at the water's edge to talk to a colleague farther back on the island. And so it was that Tom Ryssel walked first into the water, to wade back to shore.

Three steps in and he could have sworn he had placed his lower leg into some sort of an iron trap or snare. It was not painful, really just this feeling of immense pressure. It was strange that anyone would place a trap here. But then he was upended, swept from his feet, and, with his butt bumping the shallow bottom, he began sluicing rapidly through the water, almost as if being towed by a speedboat. He had three thoughts. This is a croc. I should jab its eyes. Louis will come and get me.

But his friend Louis Olivier was not quick to the rescue. Louis had been putting away some fishing tackle when he heard Tom call out and fall into the water and begin splashing about. This was the fellow who would be his best man in a few days, and Louis thought it a sick and inappropriate joke for a ranger to make with the families present, and he meant to have a word with him.

But then Louis and the others saw Tom moving through the water impossibly fast. The crocodile began spiraling, twisting Tom in ways that humans simply don't bend, and the rangers knew. They all saw the crocodile then. It was enormous. At least a thousand pounds, they figured.

There would be no saving Tom if the croc reached its destination. As soon as the croc got the ranger into deep water, it could easily drown its prey.

But then Tom reached out and jammed his fingers and thumbs into the eyes of the crocodile. The eye pokes made the crocodile swerve away from the direction of the jabs and back toward the island. Here, the predator had two disadvantages: shallow water and its grip on the ranger. The dentition of crocs lends itself to holding large prey, not killing it outright. Teeth do not penetrate the way a lion's canines might to reach and rip through spinal cords or arteries. This particular croc no doubt had killed mammals far larger than a ranger, and its jaws easily could crush smaller animals or a man, if the grip was right. But to kill most larger mammals, it needed deep water so that it could drown its prey by taking it to the bottom. There, crocs often perform a death spiral, twirling about rapidly until the disoriented prey drowns.

At the very least, this croc needed to submerge Tom's head, but its grip on Tom was on his lower legs. The croc had poor leverage, and the ranger was doing a good job of keeping his head up and out of the water. In this knee-deep part of the stream, with its hold so far down on Tom's body, the crocodile simply could not get Tom's head underwater.

After the eye gouge, the big animal lay still and seemed to Tom to be considering its next move. All the while it held tightly to Tom's legs. Then it began again moving toward deeper water.

Louis meanwhile came to understand the true situation and anticipated the croc's move. He ran down the island and then into the water to block the crocodile's path to the deeper parts of the Sabi. When the crocodile kept coming anyway, Louis improbably tackled the creature, grabbing it about its body between its front and rear legs. With strength he later could not explain, he stopped the croc and turned the half-ton creature back toward shallow water, all the while holding on to the animal.

The croc accelerated its swim and scramble through the shallows, and the three of them—the croc, Tom, and Louis—were all moving at such a high speed that the water seemed to roar past the men's ears.

Generally, a battle between a crocodile and any large mammal is determined by terrain. In deep water, the crocodile is king; on land, a mammal such as a man or a lion might have the edge. Here, the terrain of shallow water was halfway between land and deep water. The croc could still drown the prey, but the men could maneuver well enough without having to swim. In sum, it was an even playing field: neither the croc nor the men had a clear advantage.

On the plus side for the men were social bonding, teamwork, tools, and the inventiveness and adaptability of the human mind. Louis attacked with the only tool he had. Still holding on to the animal, he fumbled for his pocketknife. He then moved under the crocodile and sought out the softer underbelly. Actually, there is no soft underbelly on a croc. The little knife was useless. He threw it away in disgust. He grabbed hold of the crocodile once again, his arms around its midsection as it swam and scrambled in the shallows with his friend in its jaws.

"Mobbing" is often used as a defense against predators by hominids ("Males should mob or attack predators since they are the more expendable sex," says one text on the matter.[29]) And so it was this day. Others were joining the fray. Hans Kolver, a pilot, jumped into the water next to the crocodile's head, and Tom shouted at him to attack the croc's eyes. Kolver did, sticking his fingers into the eyes of the animal as if in an old Three Stooges movie. But each time he jabbed, the crocodile would savage Tom and shake him furiously. Those on shore could hear the pop and snap of the ranger's bones. Then the crocodile shifted its grip, releasing Tom's legs and seizing Tom squarely across his abdomen and back. Tom was still whole, but half of him hung out either side of the animal's jaw, like a horizontal hoagie in a hound's mouth. Now the croc had more control and better leverage to force Tom underwater.

Hans scrambled onto the back of the animal, seeking to again gouge the eyes. Tom, too, continued to fight his attacker, straining to poke at the eyes. Louis was still holding the animal's midsection, trying to slow the crocodile.

None of it was working. The croc was unstoppable. The eye pokes were annoying but just that, and the weight of three men was really nothing to the reptile. The crocodile headed for a part of the river entangled with vines and filled with reeds. There it ridded itself of Hans. He was brushed off by the overhanging vines and tree limbs. Worse, now the crocodile could pin Tom underwater, against the bank and the vegetation. With better leverage, the crocodile was able, finally, to hold Tom's head underwater, and it would be only a short time before the ranger drowned.

But Louis, holding the crocodile's midsection, saw the problem, released his grip and ran to Tom. He grabbed his friend's head and forced it up out of the water so Tom could breathe. The croc levered Tom down, Louis pulled him up. The croc held Tom down, Louis pulled his friend's head up. Then Louis moved quickly to the rear of the croc, grabbed it around the base of its tail, and again, with strength he did not know he had, dragged the struggling thousand-pound croc away from the vegetation and reeds back to clearer, shallower water.

Louis's plan, if plan it was, was to lift the croc onto shore, but that sort of strength no human has. The crocodile flicked its tail and sent Louis flying through air, as he would describe it later, "like a tattered rag."

This was enough to convince Louis that they could not handle the croc unarmed. So he ran toward Tom's car to retrieve his friend's revolver. Halfway there, he remembered they had left the revolver back at the rest camp. Why bring a weapon to a picnic?

Returning, Louis now grabbed hold of a thorn tree on the bank, extended his body, and dangled his legs toward Tom and the croc. He told his friend to grab his legs so they could lift him out. A helicopter pilot, Dickie Kaiser, joined the fray then and helped Louis pull on Tom. Hans was back in the fight as well, and all three hoisted the croc and Tom upward.

It seemed for a moment to work. The crocodile and Tom were lifted nearly clear of the water. But the croc was not letting go, and the incredible pressure of this tug-of-war was all focused on Tom. They risked literally tearing the poor ranger in two.

By this time, someone had brought the men a collapsible spade, an entrenching tool, and they began hammering on the crocodile. The croc thrashed about and knocked the spade out of Louis's hands. But in doing so, the croc rose up out of the water, fully exposing its eyes to Hans. And at that moment, Hans pushed the points of his fingers of both hands squarely into the reptile's eyes with well angled and forceful jabs.

This time it worked. The croc let go of Tom. It was over. Final and done. Hans and Louis had saved Tom.

But a half second later, the croc turned on Hans, clamped its jaws on his arm, and dove. Both croc and Hans disappeared underwater. They were moving rapidly away before anyone realized that Tom was free and Hans was caught.

Corrie Kaiser, the helicopter pilot's wife, had brought from the picnic area a substantial carving knife, which she now pressed into Louis's hand. At about the same time, the croc and Hans surfaced several meters away. "Help, he has me," Hans cried once.

The croc then shifted its grip, moving up the arm until it had Hans by the shoulder and upper arm, gaining excellent leverage to plunge the man underwater as it swam away.

But Louis, too, was moving again. Knife in hand, he ran past the croc through the shallows to cut it off from deep water. Again, the croc did not stop. Louis charged it head-on, intending to do great harm with the larger knife. But he found that it did no better than the pocketknife, bouncing off the croc's tough skin as if the blade were rubber.

Louis was, it is safe to say, in some form of altered state. As the crocodile lit out for deep water, with Hans's head under the water, its prey secure, swimming as fast as it could, Louis Olivier ran through the water and climbed astride its neck. Like a bronco rider, Louis settled himself on the croc and then raised the sturdy knife and buried three-quarters of its length into the animal's eye.

The crocodile instantly let loose of Hans.

But Louis did not let loose of the crocodile. He tightened his grip on the animal's throat with one arm and continued stabbing at the eyes as the mammal and the reptile sped downstream together. Finally, in the end, the crocodile twisted and swam in a spiraling motion and twirled. The torque of the water dislodged Louis, and the croc by then had lost its appetite for ranger and fled.

* * *

Tom watched this all helplessly, holding on to a tree. He saw that his friends were all right. Hans had a broken arm and injured shoulder but was OK. Then Tom looked at himself. He felt little pain, though he knew he should. He noticed that one foot faced directly backward, and before the others could see this, he reached down and twisted his foot and shattered leg back to a forward position. There was still no pain, really. His midsection was horribly mauled and torn open, of course, and he held himself in as if clutching a robe closed. It seemed as if he were neatening up a bit before visitors called.

His friend Louis, so superhumanly strong just moments ago, was now weak as a kitten, suffering from shock and exhaustion. He could not carry Tom, so he began dragging him along the ground to their Landie. It seemed a personal and private matter between friends. Others helped, and from there it was a chopper and a hospital and nine months of recovery for Tom, who rangered on with his friend for many years thereafter, and not surprisingly later named a son Louis.

There are four morals to this story. The first is that humans, and rangers in particular, can be incredibly brave, resourceful, loyal, compassionate, and at times, too, just careless enough.

The second is that rangers and park employees are a lot better at preserving wildlife than destroying it.

The third is that emotions—fear, loyalty, anger, hatred, love—play front and center in the relationship of predators and human prey, whether scientists can measure that factor or not.

The other moral is simply this: Eden kills.

Kruger is not a zoo, deer park, or exhibit, however placid it may seem. It is nature, or close to nature, because in the state of nature, organisms kill. Put a warthog, a meerkat, and a lion together in a Disney cartoon and you have a great song and dance routine. Do it in Kruger, and you have a well-fed lion.

Mammals, insects, reptiles, and raptors are killed and kill every day of the year at Kruger. Otherwise, Kruger would not be Kruger; it would not be wild and natural.

All the creatures of Kruger seemed in their own way aware of these rules, save one: humans do not think of themselves as animals. Some may understand clearly at moments such as birth and nursing that they are mammals. Still others may style themselves figuratively as fierce corporate predators or name a team after one. Yet hardly any of us ever see ourselves as prey.

But in Eden we are, or can be. Even highly trained rangers, those with the very best bush craft, can in an instant forget this fact and run afoul of Kruger's inhabitants. There can be times when all of modern technology and the cooperative society of humans is not enough to save lives.

Neville Edwards and Steve Gibson are descendents of this tough breed and know well the dangers. It would not be difficult at all to see them performing the same acts as Tom and Louis, one for the other. They are accustomed to a world of risk and willing to accept it as the inevitable downside of the rewarding lives they lead. If you are blessed, and can economically make a life in the wild work for you, then you accept the dangers. The risk and danger are most definitely one part of what makes them feel alive.

They know too that the roads we drive over, the plains we are viewing, are killing grounds at night for more than just warthogs and impalas. People die here regularly, and the specter of the dead young woman still haunts Edwards.

But then it was daylight and safari time in July 2002, and Edwards was working with his old friend and they could not help but laugh and smile like schoolboys playing hooky. To watch them is a study of human hunting skills and camaraderie that is as natural and entertaining as the bush itself. And to understand the situation in Kruger today with the lions, it is necessary to understand the rangers and guides, people like Neville and Steve. Men and women like them have been the architects and masons of Kruger, the molders of this particular part of "nature." Their behavior and that of others like them is the first clue in how the current situation came to be.

* * *

The two grew up in farm towns, mining communities, and the bush-land, and they learned bush skills from the locals and developed a great affection for the original Africans that transcend race or ethnic-ity. It is a long-running buddy movie, this one—think Butch and Sundance in Africa. Edwards is the extrovert, Hollywood handsome with square jaw and rugged ringlets of dark blond hair. He hatches plots in a light accent inherited from his English ancestors and refined in South Africa. The plots, the plans, the nature notes come in inter-rogatory form, begging understanding and collusion, in a manner that could be described as literate croc hunter. "The white rhino?" Edwards says, always asking, never stating. "When it goes to the bath-room? It is likely to come back to the same spot or latrine? This marks its territory?"

And Gibson—the quiet, dark-haired one with a fast-gun look that masks a gentle sense of humor and the courtliness of a Confederate officer when he is around women—will look at his old friend as if Edwards were Gracie Allen, shake his head at his friend's patter, and add, tersely, with a smile, "*Goes to the bathroom?*" mocking his friend. He says to me, "The 'latrines' are called 'middens.' Don't call them latrines in your story."

Often, in an excited moment, they break into Zulu, and Edwards, in his early forties now, will yell, in Zulu, "Nango!" and punch Gibson hard in the shoulder, as if they were still kids. Gibson will flash a cobralike stare, and then the corners of his mouth will twitch up and he will shake his head ever so slightly in appreciation and smile. When they were eight years old, the two would pack onto bicycles and head toward the local school, from miles out in the bush. Midway there, their parents would pass them in their Landie, smile, and wave. With the parents safely out of the way, the boys would turn their bikes around and head for a day in the bush, catch-ing snakes and stalking antelopes with slingshots. Parts of both men are still there—racing away from school. Both are intelligent, educated men who could make far more money in city jobs. But some part of them is anchored in the wild. They have chosen to do what they have always loved.

We talk. The miles unwind. I ask Neville what Nango! and the punch means, and he pauses and says, "Later? I have to put it in the proper context? So you will understand?"

The two men scan the bushes and grassland of Kruger, the rocks, the veld, the tracks or spoor, the dung. They talk in Zulu, then in English. We see the tracks of humans in the road, but whether bad-boy tourists outside their vehicles or refugees, we cannot tell. Both are likely to be wearing Western running-type shoes. Not even starving people cross the Kruger barefoot, if they can help it.

Then, near some rocks, Neville hisses in a whisper. "Steve! Steve! Slow! Tracks! On the right! Cheetah! No, leopard. Leopard! Leopard! Look at her! Pull left now. Look at her. Ahhh, she's beautiful. She is *beautiful*. Just *look* at her. Slow! Slow! Now? Now? If we just wait? She'll cross. I'll bet she'll cross. I know she'll cross. She wants to cross. Reverse! Yes, yes, yes, stop! She's going behind us now, she'll come behind us."

And a leopard, among the hardest of the big cats to find and the easiest to scare away, passes a whisker from our vehicle, moves to the bush on the other side of the road, and oblivious to us, twitches her tail as the squirrels and birds sound a warning. She moves. She stalks. The flipping metronome of her tail marks the moments. We watch as she hunts and then disappears into the bush without a backward look.

Tourists spend days searching for the mere glimpse of a leopard. Private game reserves that are known for leopard sightings command a premium of hundreds of dollars per visitor per day. We have found one in less than an hour and stayed with it for a full fifteen minutes. Shortly, we pass an open safari vehicle with a young Kruger guide at the wheel and ten tourists in the seats behind. He asks the two veterans if they have seen wildlife.

"Nothing much," Steve says.

"Only a leopard," Neville chirps and jerks his head in the leopard's direction.

The tourists' mouths gape open. The young guide tromps down on the accelerator and the big safari vehicle zooms away.

"Have to have a little fun," Neville says after a pause.

"He'll never find it," Steve says.

"The young guys?" Neville says in that interrogatory style that asks for understanding. "Only years in the bush gives you experience? He's not going to see what we see? Won't for years."

That is the sort of skill the two men have, an example of why mankind does indeed generally fare better in the overall contest with lions. Good teamwork, bonding, good bush craft, good sense, and good technology mean both men could probably survive a walk through Kruger unarmed. Armed, they could handily stalk and kill anything threatening to them, including lions.

But they don't. At one point, deep into reading about the exploits of great white hunters of years gone by and their face-offs with charging man-eaters, I ask Gibson what it was like to kill his first lion. I assume, it must be a rite of passage growing up in the bush. He is silent and grimaces slightly, as if he has bitten down too hard on one side of his mouth.

"You've never killed one?" I say finally.

He shakes his head.

"Never?"

"Why," he says, "would I ever want to kill a beautiful animal like a lion?"

"Why would I want to kill anything I cannot eat?" he asks after a pause.

This is not anomaly, and he is not playing to my greenness. Gibson is as tough as they come, not some vegan holy man. He was conscripted into an elite military unit in his youth and knows any number of ways to kill any number of animals or people. But the philosophy of most rangers is to use their skills to observe and appreciate wildlife and leave the wildlife and the ecosystem unharmed. They are a special breed—not "green" in the hyperpolitical sense. Both Neville and Steve are licensed professional hunters and will guide hunters they believe are ethical hunters. If hunting is managed correctly, they believe, then it can sustain nature. "Nature" isn't really natural here if humans do not play some predatory role. And some serious conservationists make the case that hunting paradoxically gives endangered animals an economic value that will ensure their existence. (Other conservationists of the Muir school argue the reverse position as adamantly.)

But Neville and Steve would just as soon guide as hunt. They love wild animals and nature without having to look at them over the sights of a rifle. They have a wonder of the wild. They represent a new generation of modern managers and rangers.

This notion of theirs—of conserving species that have been sworn evolutionary competitors of mankind for the alpha predator niche—is so well established on the Discovery Channel and Animal Planet and in Hollywood that we forget just how counterintuitive and recent a development it is. For thousands of years, an older paradigm rigidly ruled how humans viewed lions. And as Thomas Kuhn posits, paradigm shifts do not come without a rousing defense of the old. And the old paradigm had no use for lions at all. A hundred or so years ago, even conservationists wanted them exterminated.

How that old paradigm ended and a new lion-friendly one began was because of an array of social forces, economics, and complex emotions. But if ever there was one bridge-species between hunter and conservationist ranger in South Africa, a "missing link" between bloodthirsty meat hunter and sensitive ecologist, then the missing link would be Harry Wolhuter.

The fate of the modern lions and the Kruger rangers and guides, and the manner in which their lives, deaths, politics, and futures are intertwined, all can be seen as dating from Harry and a tale of no little drama.

For Harry was the protoranger. Without him, the park might not be, and lions might never have been saved. The story of what Harry did to the lion and what the lion did to him is a drama worth telling in full. For without the drama, without what the lion did to Harry and Harry did to the lion, and without the attendant emotion, there might very well never have been the Kruger National Park we know today.

Chapter 3

HARRY AND THE LION

A ranger in search of poaching policemen; a fall from a
horse; a terrible fate awaits; some luck and pluck; the
importance of a good lion dog; the birth of a new breed
of man.

The place where Harry Wolhuter met his lion was not far from the
spot where Neville Edwards saw the hand waving from the bush.
Both are close to the Mozambique border in the southern third of the
park. Here, high rolling hills meet the flatland of the lowveld. The
thatching grass is the dominant vegetation, with low trees spotted
here and there. Little of the terrain has changed from the day more
than one hundred years ago when Wolhuter rode by. Neville, Steve,
and I stop and stare out across the tableau toward Mozambique, and
it is not hard to imagine the scene a century back.

It had been dry in the winter of 1902, and Harry was leading a
party of pack animals, dogs, and local black African rangers in a quest
for water. Wolhuter, twenty-seven years old, tall, and as tough and
thin as the young ironwood trees that spotted the veld, was on patrol
for poachers. The rangers of the time were trying to make a statement
about preserving game, so it made no difference if the poachers were
Africans who had lived there for centuries, Afrikaners who shot for
meat, or the British who shot for sport and trophies. The poachers in
this case were thought to be police officer-sportsmen from outside the

area, which was then a game reserve, and if anything Wolhuter wanted them even more than the meat hunters or those who set out wire loops to snare and strangle passing game. The arrest of a few powerful Westerners who were also policemen who thought themselves above the law would make a strong statement that the rangers were fair and serious men, intent on stopping the slaughter of game.[30]

He had planned to halt at one water hole for the evening, but the hole was merely dust. Parched, and intent on catching the poachers, Wolhuter pressed on at night. He left alone on horseback for the next water hole and told his men to follow on foot with the pack animals. One dog, a big terrier named Bull, accompanied the ranger.

They were passing through an area that had recently been burned by numerous brush fires when Wolhuter heard animals moving. There was a velocity, a presence in the grasses that he took for antelope or some other grazer.

But then, very close to him, he saw two lions. Neither was cowed by his presence and may not even have known he was there. Both were transfixed by the horse, which they were stalking as if it were a zebra.

Wolhuter spurred the horse in an attempt to run through the lions, and he drew his rifle from its scabbard. But as he did so, one of the lions, a large male, jumped onto the back of the horse and bumped the ranger hard. The horse bucked and threw Wolhuter from the saddle.

He began his fall, rifle in hand, as the alpha predator. But the rifle tumbled from his grasp as he fell, and he landed not as a predator but as prey.

Wolhuter was now in a far worse predicament than poor Tom and Louis fighting the crocodile. In that confrontation, the social skills of humans won the day, along with the crude technology of a carving knife.

But Harry had lost *all* human advantage. His technology, the rifle, was lost in the grass, and he knew his knife, forever falling from its scabbard, was gone as well. And as for social advantage, his score there ran to negative numbers. The lions were highly socialized. There were two lions against him, and the lions were accustomed to hunting together. Wolhuter was unarmed and utterly alone.

This second lion broke the ranger's fall, then grabbed him by his right shoulder and spiked its teeth through bone, tendon, and muscle. Wolhuter felt excruciating pain and cried out. The lion, a large male, shook him as if cracking a whip. Wolhuter then remained quiet and limp. Through it all, he was aware that the horse had escaped and was pounding down the road. The first lion chased the horse. The dog, expert in harassing lions without getting mauled, chased the lion chasing the horse, assuming no doubt that Wolhuter was still astride his mount.

Wolhuter's procession was much slower than that odd race. He was being dragged to a gory, gory end as the lion searched for a nice spot to stop and begin to feed. He had seen this pageantry all too often in the bush.

Harry lay faceup toward the lion, face buried in the mane, back to the ground. His heels plowed furrows in the dirt, and each time his spurs caught, the lion worried his shoulder and growled. Wolhuter remained still, feigning death. He heard a low, purring sound from the lion, a sound of contentment not unlike that of a house cat with a mouse. The smell of the lion—"a housecat on a humid day" Capstick once called it—engulfed his senses.[31] The lion, with claws still extended, sometimes stepped on him as they moved, tearing his legs and ripping further his dangling right arm. Wolhuter, afraid the lion would stop and finish him off, remained silent even though each step brought more excruciating pain. Moreover, he was quite aware that lions regularly began eating prey while the prey still lived, usually starting on the intestines.

Even with those thoughts in mind, he was able to summon up a coolness and calmness. His right arm was crippled, but his mind was clear. He thought of a magazine article he had once read that said if you struck a house cat on the nose, it dropped what was in its mouth. He thought for a moment of trying that, but played it out in his mind. Even if the article was correct, his conclusion was always the same. Ranger hits cat on nose, cat drops prey, prey runs, cat catches and kills prey.

Plan B did not seem much better. He carried a sheath knife on his right hip—an ever so primitive piece of human technology—but he could not reach it easily. He was pretty certain it had fallen loose. He'd swiped the damn thing. Well, exchanged his old knife for it, really. He saw this fine knife in a store and the ignorant store owner was using it to cut cheese from a block on the counter. Wolhuter took his lesser knife and placed it on the cheese block, then pocketed the better knife. No one was the wiser. And he viewed it as liberating a good knife, not theft.

But the new knife was always slipping out of its sheath whenever he dismounted. The liberated knife did not fit the old sheath well. He was certain it had dislodged this time as he fell. Whenever he needed it, that knife was gone.

Slowly, with his left arm, he reached behind his back, and in a yogalike position around to his right hip. The knife was still there. He experienced near uncontrollable glee. Carefully, he gripped the handle with his left hand.

His thoughts now focused on a simple choice. Go along for the ride and succumb? Or try to do something with the sheath knife?

But try what with the knife, exactly? He could not conceive of a happy ending. Certainly, he could stick the lion and make it drop him. Then what? Certain death, he figured. The huge animal would attack him, and that would be the end of it. He could not kill a lion with a knife. But better that way, he thought. Give a fight at least. And then die quickly with a bit of honor.

The lion continued dragging Wolhuter, his boots still furrowing the dust. Then, still holding the knife, Wolhuter felt slowly, cautiously along the lion's chest until he found the pulse of a beating heart and a space between ribs.

Wolhuter's boots and spurs had plowed furrows for ninety yards. The lion would soon stop to begin feeding. So Wolhuter reached around the lion's front left shoulder, holding the knife backhanded in his left hand. He stabbed the lion twice in the chest at the pulse.

The lion roared loudly but did not drop him. Still in the lion's mouth, the ranger vibrated like a piece of waxed paper held to a comb as a kazoo. There was no Plan C, but instinctively Wolhuter swept up and stabbed at the lion's throat.

The lion dropped Wolhuter then and stood there roaring at him. The ranger scrambled to his feet, resisted the urge to run, and faced the lion.

Harry began cursing at the lion with a passion, with words he did not know he possessed. He brandished the knife and yelled at the lion, calling it all manner of names, spouting blasphemy upon blasphemy. The words vomited up from some heretofore unknown part of him.

The lion roared back and held its ground. Wolhuter braced for the charge he knew must come. Then he saw blood geysering from the lion's mane and seeping from the chest wound. The animal slumped its head as if it had suddenly grown heavy. It retreated, growling back at Wolhuter as it departed. Then the ranger could hear moans and a throaty roar that turned to a cough and then a death rattle.

Wolhuter felt an incredible sense of elation and joy and triumph—until a horrible thought occurred to him. The second lion would soon return.

It would never catch the horse now. Lions were good only for short charges. The horse no doubt had outdistanced the lion. The lion would return to the kill—to him.

Wolhuter cut off his curses. He would start a fire. He tried to set the grass on fire. Desperately, he lit match after match. But each match fizzled out. In the midst of a drought, the grass was too wet with dew.

Then he looked for trees. He must climb, he thought. But every tree he found he could not scale. His right arm was ruined, and he was weak from loss of blood. Finally, he found a scrubby tree growing at an angle. He stepped up the ramplike trunk and grasped branches with his left hand. He got out as far on one limb as he could and then lashed himself to the branch with his belt, afraid he would faint from loss of blood. He looked down. He was a scant twelve feet above the ground—a hop, skip, and a jump for a lion.

He looked down again. He could hear the second lion now, and then see it, too. The lion was following Wolhuter's blood spoor, the scent his own blood had laid down, to the tree.

Soon the second lion was looking up at him and measuring the distance to this strange piñata. If a weakened Wolhuter could climb the tree, the lion would have no trouble. The lion started up the slope of the trunk. Wolhuter yelled, cursed, and waved his arm. The lion paused. But just for a moment. Wolhuter yelled again, and the lion backed up again but not nearly as far as it had the first time.

Stone, steel, fire, knives, and guns have all helped mankind generally stay out of the jaws of lions. And to that, in Wolhuter's case, should be added one other important human advantage: the friendship and loyalty of dogs.

As Harry stared down at the lion and fought for consciousness, Wolhuter's lion dog, Bull, made some midcourse corrections. He had chased after the lion chasing the horse, and then past the lion when it gave up the chase. When the horse slowed and eventually stopped, Bull seemed finally to figure it out. The horse was riderless. The big terrier reversed direction and sprinted back to the site of the attack.

There, he found the lion halfway up the tree and Wolhuter weakly flapping his arm and yelling. The dog did not hesitate. It struck the lion hard from behind, ripping into the heels and butt of the big cat, barking and growling. The cat wheeled and Bull was gone, tail tucked in tight, sprinting just out of reach. A game of cat and dog commenced, and it was a game the dog was very good at. The rules were simple: nip, harry, and bark, but never attack for real and never close with the lion and all its superior "technology" of teeth, claws, and heft. Dogs trained by Boers—masters of guerilla warfare—did not make the mistake of directly confronting lions. Or if they did, the dog made the mistake only once.

Every time the lion started for the tree, Bull attacked from the rear. Every time the lion turned, Bull sprinted away. The dog could not kill the lion, but the lion could not catch the dog. The game went on for hours, with Wolhuter fading into unconsciousness, held high above the ground by his belt. Barks and growls and roars and yelps would awaken him. Then he would fade.

Finally, he heard the tinkle of bells on his packhorses. The "relief column" of his men had reached him and he was saved. The second lion retreated.

His rescue force thought him delirious when he said he had killed a lion with a knife. He showed them where to look for the animal's body, and the converts then helped Wolhuter walk five miles to the next water hole where, finally, he got his drink. He would ranger on for another forty-five years.

Wolhuter put Kruger and the lions of Kruger on the world map. The incredible tale was front-page news in London and worldwide, and the world suddenly was aware of the preservation effort there.

At a time when the park was young—it had been formed in 1898 as Sabi Sands Game Reserve and would not formally become Kruger National Park until 1926—and the concept of conservation just forming, the incident gave the warden, James Stevenson-Hamilton, publicity and political capital. He used it not to take vengeance on the lions that had savaged Wolhuter, but to help save the lions and other species.

It might be a stretch to say that Kruger would never have been were it not for Harry. Someone somehow might have pulled it off. But thanks to Harry and the lion, it was a lot easier. The world now knew that there was abroad in Africa a new sort of hero, the wildlife ranger who certainly could kill a lion, bare-handed with a knife if need be, but whose good angels told him the world was better served by saving animals.

The lion savaged Wolhuter horribly, but the ranger did not change into Ahab and consume his life in a quest for revenge. Be clear on this: Wolhuter was not an ecological saint. His shoulder healed poorly, but he worked on it so he could hold a rifle. Then he did wage a deadly grudge game against lions. But it was precise and brief. Then for the next four decades Wolhuter dedicated himself to preserving wildlife, and he noted proudly upon his retirement that his son would serve as a ranger, too, protecting the offspring of the lions that had nearly killed his father.[32]

The public was intrigued with Wolhuter and Stevenson-Hamilton, men who hunted down and arrested poaching police officers, not just the local natives, to save wildlife. Stevenson-Hamilton and Wolhuter leveraged that intrigue for all it was worth.

While it is oversimple to say it, these men were in a sense the first great white antihunters of South Africa. What they did changed forever the relationship of men and lions in this part of the bushveld.

Chapter 4

THE PARK SAVES THE LIONS, THE LIONS SAVE THE PARK

In order to save the lions, the new antihunters must kill them; the genius of Stevenson-Hamilton and some roots of ecology; the rangers save the lions, the lions save the park; the balance among refugees, lions, tourists, and rangers is established.

"I would like to think we are made of such stuff," Steve Gibson says one night as we talk about Wolhuter. "But the truth is I am not sure anyone is anymore."

I am not so certain about that. I think at least a bit of the social DNA of ranger Wolhuter and warden Stevenson-Hamilton is present everywhere in the park. I think it is present in the rangers, visitors, Steve and Neville, and the lions, too. I want to trace a straight line from the current social DNA of the tourists, of the rangers, and of Neville and Steve back to where Harry walked away from his lion. But a small detour down a slightly curvy path of my safari is needed to give context to the present, its participants, and the past.

Neville, Steve, and I linger for a while near the spot where Wolhuter rose to glory. Ours is a much easier trip than his. There is no real roughing it for us and no need for it. We stay within the fenced camps of Kruger at night in spare but comfortable concrete buildings that resemble thatched African huts—only with plumbing. In the mornings, we eat breakfast in a park concession, then drive the roads of Kruger, eat a packed lunch, then head back into a secure Kruger camp for dinner and the evening.

My whole family is in Africa again, just in different spots at different times. Suzanne, my wife, who is a photographer, has her own photographic safari scheduled and will also join Steve, Neville, and me for part of her stay. Sarah, my daughter, then an adventurous seventeen-year-old, is about to take a three-week university course on game rangering in the wilds just west of Kruger. Ever the good parents, we arrive with Sarah and ask the professor if we can inspect her tent and see the camp.

"Not a great idea now," he says in a whisper, nods toward the tent, and moves his hands down in a dampening motion. "Bull elephant in musth, I'm afraid. Shouldn't really go much closer or make any fast movements now."

We gaze over and indeed there is a huge tusker sniffing at the entrance of a camp tent. Suzanne and I exchange dubious glances. Sarah says aloud to herself in a slow, quiet voice, "This . . . is going to be . . . so great." We leave her there with a sexually aroused and cranky elephant, assurances from the professor, and a cell phone that may or may not work in this part of the bush.

As we drive on, my thoughts are more on Sarah in the tent, and I feel a long way from any danger of confronting any lions. Still, when I get out to water a bush, both Steve and Neville post themselves on watch at opposite ends of the compass. They are looking earnestly for any dangers. Once we are outside the cars, we are exposed. There is no joking here, and my one attempt falls flat; they do not drop their eyes from surveillance, and they do not laugh or speak. They are deadly serious, and the dangers are real.

Ecotourism is seen as a future growth industry in South Africa, as is hunting, although it is less emphasized. Both Steve and Neville—the spiritual descendants of Wolhuter—are members of professional hunting associations that oppose the canned hunts often held for trophy hunters. There are lion farms in South Africa, and antelope farms as well, where Americans and Europeans will pay up to $50,000 to "hunt" an animal in an enclosed space. A friend of mine signed up to hunt a valuable antelope "trophy," not knowing just how canned the hunt was.

Said my friend: "There were maybe thirty acres surrounded by a white fence, no brush or undergrowth or cover, and the dark antelope was clearly outlined anywhere it went. I told the guy who ran it I wanted a hunt, not an execution, and walked away from it." Others make a distinction between "hunters" of wild lions and "shooters" of canned lions. Hunters have great disdain for shooters.[33]

Shooters seem to think scruples were a vegetable they scraped to the side of the plate as kids. The BBC a few years back ran an exposé of hunters shooting from cars at lions who were so domesticated they had to be shooed away before being shot. The tame lions wanted their ears scratched. Other "guides" would market the black-market thrill of killing a real Kruger lion. Reportedly, they cut holes in the Kruger western fence, stake out a ripe zebra or antelope, and lure a park lion pride out for clients who blaze away.

My friend Tom Masland also wrote about the abuses in *Newsweek*. A son of the American South, he knew and respected ethical hunters. He found few ethical hunts in South Africa in his reporting, but plenty of canned ones.

"Lions may suffer the most," he wrote. "A big lion with a bushy black mane can bring in $25,000, a rare white lion more than twice that. And South Africa is the only place to get one easily. . . . captive breeding operations—the equivalent of puppy mills—are the inevitable results."[34]

Steve and Neville condemn the sort of "sport" that does not contain "fair pursuit." There are game ranches in Africa that run ethical hunts. Steve also often guides in other countries in bush where a true hunt still can be had. Moreover, they have found a large part of their business is in guiding tourists on viewing or photographic safaris.

They have had some high-profile clients. When the Hollywood movie *Ghost and the Darkness* was filmed in South Africa, Neville showed star Michael Douglas around the park. Both Steve and Neville's businesses were family-based, with Neville and his wife working out of Nelspruit near the park running a bed-and-breakfast in tandem with the safari business. Steve and his wife, Sharon, formed Esseness Safaris farther south in Empangeni.

Somewhere along the line the relationship between Neville and his wife went south, and they divorced. Before we started the safari, he had a brief afternoon with his kids. The youngest daughter of about age six clung to his knee and beamed out at passersby with the happy smile of a cat having eaten a dozen canaries. His older daughter, about twelve, talked with her father with a presence and grace that seemed beyond her years—a young, swan-necked Audrey Hepburn in her beauty. Neville's ex stood nearby, smiling at the scene. She now runs her own tourist travel business. Whatever the cause of the parting, the postdivorce seems to be working out. Dad and daughters have a wonderful connection, it is clear.

But Neville's dream of a family-owned business is on the rocks, and so is his life of working in the bush. He has a first-rate job as director of a Zulu cultural center, but that is not the same as guiding. For this trip, he needed to take vacation leave to team up with Steve.

"Not to sound mean about it," he says as we cover dozens of miles in the bush, "and I don't know how to say it other than that the divorce took everything. I'm starting over."

In a way, he has had to "go corporate." There is a sense that this joint safari with Steve—not a common thing for them—is also a good time for bonding and buddy talk that might get Neville over the hump of being single and removed from the bush life he loves.

"What you should really write about," Neville says more than once, "is not just the parks and the lions, but the *relationships*, the *friendships* that endure through the *toughest* time, the love and the bonds people form."

A short time later Neville yells, "Nango!" again, and Steve is braced for the punch and already smiling. This trip with his old wing-man may be doing more for Neville than adding a few of my dollars to his bank account. The old stories, the retelling of the tales, is a shoring up of old bonds and, it seems, of Neville himself.

Certainly old stories are in abundance. There was the time when they were just ten, known to everyone in the town and the bush from tribesmen to tradesmen as amusing little terrors who streaked through town and the bush on bicycles wreaking harmless havoc. They would appropriate the coupons from front-porch bottles and enjoy the thick, cream-topped milk from local dairies. Then it was off to a nearby dam that formed a large reservoir and lake.

"I think it was the danger factor," Steve wrote me later. "Playing with our destiny—according to our own set of bush rules that attracted us to the dams because these dams were complete with pythons and crocodiles. Yet we used to swim, kayak, and fish in these dams all the time."

Their *own* set of bush rules. They were not suicidal. They did not jump into a croc-filled lake. They watched, they learned, they observed. They took calculated risks. Some of their adventures were mischievous, even vandalistic. They were deadly with slingshots and would pepper the local buses with small stones, or sometimes sniper out a window of an empty bus with an air gun.

But there was a valor, too, and not just the sort that set them swim-ming with crocs and pythons at age ten. Come night, they would creep into the bush and find the camps of poachers. As the adult men, all armed, slept, Steve and Neville would collect the poachers' snares and illegal fishing nets, carry them away, and destroy them.

Their own set of bush rules. They might carry off the poachers' nets one day, but refuse to inform on them another. The two boys were known to hang out at the dam, and so when a farmer found that twenty-one of his ducks had been poached from the lake formed by the dam, Neville and Steve became the suspects. The community, their parents, the tribesmen all accused Steve and Neville. They took the fall—groundings and restitution. They knew the real perpetrator but have not given him up to this day. They could not, under their set of bush rules. Was he a black African friend? I speculate. Would he have had worse punishment than you? My query is met by smiles and the silence imposed by bush rules.

Soon Steve and Neville were traveling widely with Gibson's father, a miner and prospector. And there were trips with a family friend, Mike Edwards, a government game and tsetse fly control officer. Sometimes, the trips lasted three or four weeks, and the men and boys were totally immersed in remote bush. They needed to shoot meat for themselves and their considerable entourage of policemen, trackers, and bearers. It was here that Gibson learned tracking and hunting skills that would last him a lifetime. He began the trips when he was ten. At age twelve, under the direction of officer Edwards and to protect a village's crops and provide meat, Steve killed his first elephant.

If Neville is in postdivorce, out-of-the-bush hangover mode, his time with Steve seems curative. His skills as a guide and naturalist need no restoration at all. He points out game I would have missed on either side of the road, or stops to show us various tracks or sign.

Nowhere in this region do we see a monument to Harry or his lion. And of course there is no monument for the woman Neville saw that day in July 2000. The question I have on my laptop computer screen is how the men like Wolhuter preserved the park and a culture that preserves men like Neville and Steve, as well as the lions. I need to find that straight line of social DNA running from Wolhuter and Stevenson-Hamilton to Edwards and Gibson. The answer comes just a little way down the road, and the line linking Steve and Neville to the past becomes straighter and clearer.

We pass by a monument, some twenty feet tall, carved of a rock in a smaller but still grand imitation of Mount Rushmore. The visage is that of Paul Kruger, one of the most famous Afrikaners.

But as is sometimes common in research, it is what's missing that is most telling. It was Kruger who proposed legislation for the first reserve, but in fact, if statues were built in proportion to the size of contribution made to the park, warden James Stevenson-Hamilton would command the Rushmore-like status and Kruger would be more a bookshelf bust. This fact is only now being more widely recognized in the postapartheid era because Kruger was an Afrikaner legend and Stevenson-Hamilton was a Brit—a Scot to be precise. So for years, Stevenson-Hamilton's contribution was downplayed.

From the start, he seemed an odd candidate to become one of the most influential conservationists of the century. He stood only five foot four, nearly a foot shorter than Wolhuter, and was an avowed trophy hunter.

He would have been surprised as well, for he had little idea what lay ahead for him in July 1902 as he crossed the Sabi River into what is now Kruger National Park. There was no real sign that he had crossed into a game reserve, for that matter. There were no animals. No lions. No antelopes. No zebras or giraffes. Not even tracks or sign that he could see or spin a tale around.[35]

But of all the things that James could not see on that day, the most significant was that the river for him, at age thirty-five, was one of those markers of personal history or mythology that once crossed set destiny—for him, the next forty-four years of his life.

Instead, James Stevenson-Hamilton, sporting a dapper beard and immaculately trimmed mustache, was at times gently grumbling to himself, as he often did, debating internally whether he had done the right thing or the wrong thing about this or about that.

The thoughts, recorded in his diary, went like this: he should have stayed in Scotland and revived his estate. He should have been married by now and produced some heirs. He could have asked for more money on this job. He should have waited them out a little longer.[36]

There were only two things he knew for certain on this trip. The first was that he was absolutely at home in this wilderness, every bit as comfortable as Wolhuter was. So assured was James in the Scottish heather, in the bush, or on the battlefield that it was said men forgot his diminutive stature a half minute after meeting him.

The second sure thing he knew was the ephemeral nature of the new appointment. This wardenship of Sabi Game Reserve was nothing more than an interlude for him. He was at play, really. James was a British cavalry officer and upper-class landed gentry. He would take another turn in the army; or he would head back to his family estate, Fairholm, in Scotland. He would make a go of it there, somehow, and do something gentlemanly, even though the mines and the factories of the industrial age were even then encroaching on the Scottish heather he knew as a boy. These were the serious personal matters he pondered in his log on a regular basis.

This job was not one of those serious matters. It was a lark. He liked being outdoors. He liked the African wilderness. He liked good stories to tell, and could tell a story well. He liked being "self-reliant" and had an egalitarian respect for self-made men, so much so that it might be easy to mistake his attitude for that of an American or an Australian.

This tendency, and his unabashed pluck, was most apparent when he filed formal charges of incompetence against his commander, seeking his removal from field command during the war. The officer had botched his command and one of James's men in the ranks was killed as a result. The officer then jailed James—but for what he could not say. The commander of both James and his superior ordered them to cool off. James took leave to take the warden position.

He fingered a scrap of handwritten paper in his pocket—the only official document memorializing his "commission" as warden—as he drew nearer to the reserve. Again, he mentally kicked himself for accepting too soon. The job paid five hundred pounds a year. If only he "had had the sense to ask for it," the man would have gone six hundred, James later wrote in his journal.[37]

The reserve had existed since 1898, just before the Boer War began, but truth be told the war had delayed any real preservation of game. In fact, both sides, the Boers and the Brits, shot the game for provisions. But the man who hired him noted that James was so "brimful of pluck and resource" that he thought Stevenson-Hamilton might actually accomplish something.[38]

So first James took leave from the 6th Inninskilling Dragoons.

Then he crossed the Sabi River and forever and completely for the rest of his life took leave of his senses.

"The Sabi 'witched' me away from the world," he would write in his log of what was then known as the Sabi Reserve. "The Sabi is a courtesan and her delight kept me in dalliance."[39]

Later, he would try to describe what had entranced him so that first day.

The sun, low in the west, is gilding the bare pinnacle of Logogote, and is lending fleeting shades of delicate pink to the three peaks of Pretorious Kop—border beacons of the land of mystery beyond.

Eastwards, far as the eye can see, stretches a rolling expanse of tree tops, in the foreground a medley of green, yellow and russet brown but with increasing distance merging into a carpet of blue-gray. . . . Wildlife is just awakening from its afternoon siesta. Francolins are calling around, and from a nearby donga comes the sudden clatter of a guinea-fowl; bush babblers are chattering among the trees, their cheerful din serving to render yet less definable the vague sounds which here and there are beginning to rise from the distant forest.

It is the voice of Africa, and with it comes to me a sense of boundless peace and contentment.[40]

The new job came at a time when he had spent years in military service, had served years fighting the inglorious Boer War, had suffered for years seeing his men die and witnessing the deeds of stupid commanders at work. At home in Great Britain, the mines and industrialization relentlessly closed in on the old family estate. He found the solitude and autonomy of the African wilderness invigorating and wrote once of it: "This life just suits me."[41]

Once smitten by the Sabi, James traveled through its far nooks and crannies, just as intensely as he had the family estate in Scotland as a young boy. Carts and wagons pulled by oxen with James riding ahead on horseback would forge through the bushland for weeks at a time as he surveyed and mapped and took a census of animals and man. But more than the game, more than the lions, more than the birds or the snakes or other reptiles or the people, it was the sheer sense of place that charmed him.

Soon, as he was wont, he began to see the area in terms of a system. Perhaps it was the military strategist in him. But it was not the first time he had thought this way. While hunting earlier in his life, once with Theodore Roosevelt, he was distraught to see areas ravaged by overhunting, by agriculture, by herding. But when he came to a "natural" spot, an area untouched by civilized man, an area large enough for the animals to migrate and move about, he felt great joy. He saw how the animals and the grasses and the trees and the predators and the prey all were connected, swaying together naturally in an exquisitely balanced mobile of natural forces—what years later would be seen as a balanced ecological system.

And that, he thought, was what was needed here. He had made the conversion from hunter to naturalist at Sabi, and his daily notes and observations were serious, intense. They led him to one conclusion: the reserve must grow, must become much larger, and must in fact be huge to allow the more natural range and migrations of the prey and their predators.

And so resolved, James would stop at nothing to realize his plans.

The expansion came easily in some ways. It was worthless land, after all. Tsetse flies swarmed over livestock, oxen, and horses. These foreign mammals died by the thousands. Only three or four horses in a hundred showed immunity to the sickness. Malaria plagued the human settlers in the summer months. The land could not be worked, so the land companies willingly placed their untilled acres under the reserve's care. Soon land was assembled, quite larger than all of the Netherlands.

But the challenge was not in gaining the land. The challenge was in policing it. Scraps of paper in one's pocket did not make a reserve, particularly when the regular police outside the reserve, the constabulary, defied the entire concept of game rules, and sponsored armed social outings.

James and Wolhuter, his first hire, soon decided they needed to change that state of affairs. The two sat down and plotted it, the ranger a full head taller than his boss. They needed a test case, an example, to show they were serious. The idea of chasing the privileged white policemen poaching on the land was Stevenson-Hamilton's, but it was thoroughly embraced by Harry.

However, when the lion caught Harry instead of Harry catching the hunters, James was concerned on a number of levels. The high officials certainly had escaped capture and punishment that day. And poor Wolhuter needed months of rehabilitation.

The upside was the worldwide attention. Yes, the stories were sensational and emotional. But they focused the world on Stevenson-Hamilton's efforts. And then, later, James nailed the police poachers of the South African Constabulary, brought them to trial, and convicted them.

"Enough to make one chuck one's job," James wrote in his log after their arrest, fully anticipating "a travesty of justice." But when they received stiff fines, the rest of the lowveld and most of Africa were jolted by this celebrated and precedent-setting case.[42] This was not a native-bashing warden who blamed the indigenous Africans. Nor was Stevenson-Hamilton a poseur, giving the wink and nod to his countrymen-sportsmen, while hunting regularly himself. He drove straight and directly toward the local power structure—and broke its back. Poachers, even if they were white policemen, now knew they had their very own predators chasing them.

Then, in 1910, with a foreword by Teddy Roosevelt, Stevenson-Hamilton published *Animal Life in Africa*, a book that was part an explanation of what would become known as ecology and part a highly emotional adventure story of preserving game by chasing down poachers and, yes, hunting for lions. It was a worldwide best seller and established James as one of the foremost naturalists and conservationists of his time. Anytime he returned to London, he was welcomed at the wood-paneled clubs where he could recount his close calls and encounters in the wild.

The other quarry James chased was lion. Even after his conversion, he really had no choice.

Conservationists at the end of the nineteenth century often were so-called repentant butchers—hunters who had seen the light. They worked to save the very animals they once had shot in great numbers. The antelope, the buffalo, the giraffes, and wildebeests, all had shrunk to perilously low levels.

The conservation effort that set out to save the valued game did this—logically, so it seemed—by eliminating anything that killed the favored game species. Hence, poachers were arrested and sports hunting prohibited.

The same policy held true for other animals that killed the favored animals, but in this case "elimination" was the literal goal.

Carnivores that preyed on the game species were held in the utmost contempt. Crocodiles were described by one conservationist as nothing more than "animated traps that should be exterminated."[43] The same held true for leopards, hyenas, smaller carnivora, raptors, and, in particular and especially, the lion. They were all considered unneeded and in a real sense evil villains.

This had been the prevailing thought and had been for centuries. In the epic poem *Beowulf*, the monster was not just another Joe trying to make his way in the world who just happened to stop at the mead hall for some fast food and a thane to go. It was evil. The Seamus Heaney translation of *Beowulf* puts it this way:

In off the moors, down through the mist bands
God-cursed Grendel came greedily loping.[44]

Like Grendel, the lion was seen not as a normal animal or even an undesirable animal. It was God-cursed. Greed, not the natural order of things, propelled lions. The animal's rank at the top of the food chain meant it was even more evil and accursed than the other carnivores.

So lions were shot on orders even by the rangers. Everyone agreed this was the right thing to do. The Boers, the Brits, the Africans. The ethnic groups often could agree on little. But they agreed on this. Lions were like big rats. They were to be trapped, poisoned, run down by dogs, ambushed by trip guns, speared, snared, and hunted from horseback until they were gone for good.[45]

Nearly everyone believed this, that is, except Stevenson-Hamilton, the head of what was then called Sabi Sands Game Reserve.

He saw it differently and instinctively grasped the essence of ecology. Almost from the beginning, he believed that lions served a useful purpose in keeping nature in balance and that they should be left alone. Otherwise, Kruger would be little more than an artificial "deer park." The antelope, zebras, wildebeests, and giraffes needed predators to keep everything in balance.

But even Stevenson-Hamilton could not stop killing lions in the political climate of the early twentieth century. He was attempting his own paradigm shift of how predators were viewed, and he had no shortage of opposition. Preserve managers frequently were attacked by ranching interests as "creating a breeding ground for lions."[46] The sportsmen wanted antelope protected. The two groups were politically dominant, and even the greens of the time agreed. They all demanded an aggressive campaign of lion extinction so the "game" could live.

Said Kruger ranger and author G. L. Smuts in his book, *Lion*, written in 1982, "Stevenson-Hamilton and his staff were not popular and a general hate campaign was being waged against their conservation policy. . . . Public opinion was . . . strongly anti-carnivore and in 1905, speaking at a meeting of the Transvaal Game Protection Society, a Mr. Kirby stated: 'the Reserve is simply a lion breeding concern, and not a protection for game.'"[47]

Twenty years later, the criticism and hatred was little changed. "I would like to draw to your readers' attention the scandal of the Sabi Game Reserve, where they have been breeding lions for the last twenty years," said a 1925 letter to the editor of *Farmer's Weekly*.[48] The writer estimated that five thousand to ten thousand lions were in the reserve. At the time, Stevenson-Hamilton counted only six hundred.

It would not have taken a terribly aggressive campaign to eliminate the lions in 1902. Some said there were only nine lions in the whole park then, and the highest estimate was just thirty.[49]

What saved them was Stevenson-Hamilton's showmanship and sleight of hand. Like Steve and Neville, he had his own set of bush rules. He would kill lions when necessary to appease political interests and ranchers. He would do this with great fanfare and publicity and stage photos of lion skulls and proclaim himself a great lion killer. Old photos show row upon row of bleached-out lion skulls with their fanged overbites. The remains are lined up by size like a grim class picture.

In fact, he and the rangers did kill a lot of lions. Said ranger/author Smuts: "The number of lions officially killed inside the park between 1902 and 1969 was 3,031."[50]

But often Stevenson-Hamilton ordered "show killings" as a political necessity. And at times, hunter that he was, he also killed lions. He would claim later to have personally dispatched more than one hundred fifty of them. Those deeds immunized him against charges of being soft on lions. Always, though, he was careful to make sure enough lions remained to keep the species alive. Park officials years later would conclude that only this benevolent deception saved the lion from extinction in South Africa.

A key element, Smuts noted, was not what Stevenson-Hamilton did, but what he did *not* do.

"Annual reports show that although the accepted policy was to destroy large carnivores, few were actually shot during the first year of the Sabi Game Reserve." Smuts noted, "In these early years it was also policy to keep all carnivorous reptiles and even predatory birds in the reserve within reasonable limits. At no stage, however, was the aim to eliminate a species but rather to reduce the impact of predators in general. In addition to boosting depleted game numbers, the carnivore control programme served an important public relations function with regard to irate neighbors and landowners who wanted more lions to be shot."[51]

So the lions survived and mated and grew under Stevenson-Hamilton, but they were still considered a less than desirable species even two decades later. The reserve still existed only for sportsmen, and the thought was that at some future date—Stevenson-Hamilton stalled and stalled as to when exactly—hunters would finally be allowed to enter the preserve, and their fees would pay for the reserve. The government was growing restless subsidizing it.[52]

Stevenson-Hamilton found another way. In the 1920s, he persuaded a railroad to schedule a stop near what is now called Skukuza—the park's current governing center and ranger headquarters. The railroad company was already running passenger train tours of South Africa, and Stevenson-Hamilton begged them to simply add a few hours in Kruger. Tourists would go out in carriages and view the antelope and gawk at the giraffes.

But as it turned out, the tourists found then, as they do now, that the main draw was not "game" as the white hunter defined it. Antelope were just fine, yes, yes, but what the tourists wanted to see were the lions. Soon, the lions became the era's equivalent of radio crooners, by far the most popular draw in the park. To add a little touch, some of Stevenson-Hamilton's staff would dress up in lion skins and scare the bejeebers out of the tourists as they sat around a campfire. Others were saying, yes, they had seen elephants, giraffes, zebras, buffalo, leopards, and a rhino, but the trip was a complete failure without seeing lions. Where were the lions? They had come for the lions![53]

The park, which is to say the lions of the park, was the most popular part of the train stops. And soon, as more roads were hacked through the wilderness, came the logical thought of expanding access to the park to automobiles.

There was one catch in the "car theory." No one, including Stevenson-Hamilton, knew what would happen when tourists in cars met actual lions—particularly if cars entered the park unescorted. For the most part, by the 1920s the lions had lost just about all fear of humans. So long as most contact was during the daytime, everything seemed fine. The lions were "habituated" to humans—used to them.

"Stevenson-Hamilton was also aware that once lions had been hunted during the day and one or more had been wounded or killed, the others generally became shy and often confined their activity to the hours of darkness, subsequently become valueless to the now important [tourist draw]," Smuts wrote. So when the park was formally chartered as a national park in 1926, Stevenson-Hamilton officially halted the killing of lions. In other words, Stevenson-Hamilton encouraged the habituation so lions would not shy away from the road. He wanted them to be comfortable with humans nearby.[54]

Good things can come of that, and very bad things as well. Just a few years back, a British college student on safari in Africa forgot to tie down his tent flap. He awoke in the night with a lion staring at him from a foot away. He did what most of us would do: he ran. Whether the lions were looking for food or, more likely, just curious, the running triggered the reflexes of the lion in the tent and the pride outside, and the youth was caught and killed.[55]

About this time, on my safari, this particular bit of research comes back to me, and I think of my daughter in a tent west of Kruger. Because she was the only young woman in the class, the professor assured me that she would have her own tent. That seemed nice then, crazy now. I try her cell phone and leave a message. Twenty minutes later she calls back, slightly out of breath.

"Did you get my message about the tent?" I ask.

"Yeah," she says, "sorry, I have to catch my breath . . . I'm thirty feet up a tree . . . the only place I can get good cell reception. There's this one spot . . . "

Cute of me to be concerned, she says, reminds me that she is smart and no one's fool and handles guys just fine. First night out, she appeared at the next tent over, cot and clothes in hand. "Hi, guys," she said. "I'm your new roommate. I get dressed over in that tent, sleep over here. No problems? Great, this place looks about right."

She sets up in the back of the tent. There are three college-age Afrikaner boys; two are each roughly the size of a Coke vending machine. My worries for her recede but do not disappear. Always in the wild, you manage your risk and hedge your bets, but habituation has brought trouble for even veteran rangers.

My worries are not helped by the 1972 story documented by Capstick of a lion pride that had taken to killing chickens in a safari camp.[56] They were within the borders of Wankie National Park in what then was Rhodesia. Nothing could be done to the lions unless they attacked humans, and they did not seem prone to that—just the occasional chicken. The lions seemed habituated but harmless.

At the camp were Len Harvey, an experienced game warden, and his new wife, Jean. They were honeymooning and stayed in a mud hut. Nearby was another ranger, Willie De Beer. His wife, daughter, and her husband, a young college student named Colin Matthews, stayed in another hut.

Both parties were armed with quite adequate rifles, but because of rebel activity at the time the rifles were required to be locked away. No one was terribly concerned about the lions, and the chickens were no big loss.

But it seemed that at least one lioness had associated the spot with food, and at around 11 P.M., as the Harveys slept, the lioness hopped through the window of the mud hut. It attacked Jean, biting her through the small of her back. She cried out, waking Len. There was no flight in this situation, only fight. He attacked the lioness. With no weapons, he punched, scratched, and wrestled.

The lioness left Jean and turned on Len Harvey. He yelled to his wife to run, and she did. Halfway to the De Beer hut, she stopped and turned back, thinking to help. And as Capstick put it, "the sound that came through the darkness left no doubt that Len Harvey was beyond help."

In their underwear, De Beer and his young son-in-law unlocked and loaded two rifles. De Beer made sure the safety was on. He took the heavier .375 H&H and gave Matthews the lighter .243 Parker Hale—a smaller caliber but with a very high velocity. The veteran ranger carefully cased the hut where the lion lay. He sneaked up to peer inside the window. He thought about firing blindly into the hut, but feared Len might still be alive. He slipped off his safety and cautiously called Len's name. Nothing. Still, he felt he needed to see the lion before he shot. He knew it was all too common in these situations for helpful hunters to kill a human rather than the lion.

He stuck his head and the rifle into the hut window and saw Harvey's legs, still and covered in blood. It was at this time that the lioness batted out a paw and sliced De Beer's forehead to the bone. Shocked by the pain, blinded by his own blood, he fell back. Then he asked Matthews to tie a ripped T-shirt around his wound. It kept the blood out of his eyes and back went De Beer, intent on dispatching the lioness.

He was more cautious this time, but the lioness was bolder. As he neared the window, the cat reached out with a paw and caught him behind the head, drawing him forward toward her jaws. She was trying for a bite on the skull, which would take care of De Beer for good. The ranger yelled and in agony dropped his gun inside the hut. Then he pulled away with such force that the lion's claws came loose—but only after leaving deep grooves in De Beer's scalp and pulling it forward. Blinded by his own blood and hair, he teetered backward and fell. The lioness this time jumped through the window to finish the job.

De Beer was nearly unconscious and completely sightless now, but he knew to cover his head with his arms. The lioness bit down on his arms and began to drag him away. She chewed as she dragged, the bones in De Beer's hands and arms breaking under the pressure.

Just a few feet away, young Colin Matthews watched the grisly scene. He had never hunted. He did not know guns, or know that a "safety" existed. He tried but could not fire the rifle. He struggled to help his father-in-law as best he could, and then literally put his foot into a bucket. He fell then, and so did the rifle.

The lioness looked up to see what was causing the racket and charged Matthews head-on. His foot was still jammed into the bucket when the lioness was upon him, and he instinctively put his right arm into the animal's mouth and grabbed its tongue.

His arm, of course, was mauled and broken quickly. Neither man seemed to have much chance now. Neither had a gun. Both were terribly wounded.

But the semiconscious and still sightless De Beer could hear the struggle nearby and groped about until he found the barrel of the rifle that Matthews had dropped. He pulled on it, but it was stuck. The lioness in fact was standing on it. He yanked it free somehow, slipped off the safety, and listened, trying to figure out where to shoot.

From the growls and the screams, it seemed to him that the growls were higher than the human sounds, and so that is where he shot first. Then, with broken hands, he shot twice more.

All was quiet then. The lioness slumped down, finally dead. De Beer's blind shooting had struck her first in the lungs, then in the shoulder and heart, then in the right cheek. De Beer and Matthews helped each other struggle back to the women huddled in a hut. De Beer's wife drove the three injured people thirty miles, where they were evacuated by helicopter. They survived, but Len Harvey, as they had suspected, was dead on the hut floor.

The point from that experience is simple: back in the 1920s in Kruger, *any* incident like that—*just one*—might well have sealed the fate both of the lions and of Kruger. The park and its lions still had powerful enemies who could use such a run-in to close or hamstring the park. Emotions still ran high against lions in the agricultural community, and a De Beer-like debacle could have provided the bellows to revive the smoldering coals of lion hatred and spread it burning through the politics of the country.

So it was a great risk Stevenson-Hamilton took when he allowed normal "citizens" into the park in automobiles. No one really had a clue what would happen. The earliest visitors were assigned a ranger, but volume soon made that impractical. Then it was thought that each car should carry a rifle. That too turned impractical. A loaded rifle is difficult to use in a car, and a pistol would largely be ineffective. It became apparent that the greatest danger to tourists carrying a loaded rifle in a crowded automobile was not from lions but from tourists carrying a loaded rifle in a crowded automobile.

"When it was first decided to allow tourists to enter the Park, unescorted, in their own cars, it was not known how the lions would take it," Stevenson-Hamilton wrote. "Personally, I thought it likely that they would give the roads a wide berth; being highly intelligent creatures, it was hardly to be supposed that they would deliberately put themselves in the way of possible danger.

"On the other hand, those whose ideas of them were culled from traveller's tales and nursery stories, quite naturally pictured them as ravening, homicidal maniacs, whose chief aim in life being to lap human blood, were only to likely tear our visitors from their cars."[57]

As the good warden noted, the lions proved both theories wrong.

"Having made up their minds that motor cars were neither good to eat nor a potential danger to themselves, they almost completely ignored them," he wrote.[58]

It is a phenomenon known to most tourist areas where the habituation to humans has been gradual. It allows for incredible viewing at very close range and is a good part of what makes the true tourist safari attractive, even magical.

It also is a source of debate among modern rangers to this day. Some think the lions simply do not perceive humans in the cars, unless there is motion or a human "breaks the profile" of the auto or Landie. Others say this is ridiculous. "Do you really think an animal that can spot a limping zebra from half a mile cannot distinguish you and me looking out the window?" one ranger asked.

Stevenson-Hamilton was at first convinced that the lions were dumber than he thought and that "the smell of the petrol and oil drowned the human odour; that the semi-obscurity wrapping the people inside, their heads only visible from the level of a lion's eyes, effectually concealed their identity. I became further confirmed in my belief after having tried occasionally the experiment of getting out of the car on the opposite side of it from the lions, and then suddenly showing myself in the roadway.

"When I did this the previous sleepy and unconcerned animals always sprang to their feet and with grunts of alarm made off at full gallop, indicating thus to my mind that once they recognized a human being, their natural fear of him immediately showed itself."

So lions *were* dumber than he thought. Yet Stevenson-Hamilton never was a careless observer. Nor was he arrogant enough to think that his conclusion could not be challenged, and as he wrote, "later observation led me to alter this opinion.

"There was, I began to realize, something more subtle in the lion's attitude than I had previously suspected. It is difficult, perhaps impossible, even for those who have had much contact with wild animals, to guess how their minds work or to imagine how ordinary things appear to their eyes; but it may be hazarded, since all animals judge external from their own experiences of them, that the lion perfectly well realizes there are human beings inside the cars, but, by some queer train of reasoning, never having known them to be enemies while sitting in one, thinks that, so long as they stay like that, they remain automatically friendly, but the moment they get out, they resume their natural hostile role.

"Sometimes I have got out on the running-board and seen the lions spring up ready to bolt, only once more to lie down quietly the moment I again re-entered the car," he said.

So there it was. A small observation in field zoology from a man with no formal scientific training, and yet one that had enormous impact on Kruger and all other parks and future ecotourist resorts. These lions, during the daytime, were habituated enough to permit incredibly close access by automobile or Land Rover. They knew humans were present but judged that they posed no danger.[59]

Or so it seemed. And so it almost always was. Stevenson-Hamilton noted that the only serious injury to a tourist was one who had disembarked from his auto. And the injury—a serious goring—came from a sable antelope, not a lion.

The lions from the start were the draw. "To the majority of the visitors the main, one might even say the sole, attraction of the Park has been the lions," Stevenson-Hamilton wrote. And it could be frustrating for him at times, as it would be to any naturalist.

"When two cars meet on the road and the occupants stop to exchange news," Stevenson-Hamilton said, "the first mutual question invariably is, 'Did you see a lion?' sometimes, 'Did you see anything?' which has the same implication. I once asked a man if he had come across much along the road. 'Not a blessed thing,' he replied. 'But,' I said, rather surprised, 'I have just been along there myself, and I saw any number of impala, some waterbuck, and a few rather fine sable antelope.' 'Oh, those,' was the contemptuous rejoinder; 'yes, I saw *them* all right, but I did not see a single lion!'"[60]

Kruger National Park, James Stevenson-Hamilton, and the lions had by the late 1920s created the two essential ingredients for survival: a political mandate and funding. But what Stevenson-Hamilton needed as the automobile age dawned and prospered was roads and bridges to give even more tourists even more access. And here he found another unique solution.

For decades, Mozambicans had traveled across the park to the mines and fields of South Africa. The Shangan tribesmen in particular were prized workers. There were few problems with Mozambicans and lions in this era because the workers traveled in daytime and because Shangan were "bush smart," said by some to be the world's best trackers. The Portuguese government, which "owned" Mozambique, in effect would rent out the workers. Close to 100,000 legal workers would cross the park each year. But the colonial government also required the workers to pay the Portuguese for a permit. Many workers sought to avoid these payments by simply crossing the park. Mine owners were only too happy to receive them—and avoid the fee they had to pay to the Portuguese government.[61]

It was this set of affairs that prompted another spark of genius from Stevenson-Hamilton. As the Mozambicans crossed the park, he would detain them. He would give the workers a choice: work on building roads for two weeks in the park and obtain an official work permit from him for the mines, or get the work permit by spending two weeks in jail.

Most of the Mozambicans welcomed the deal. They actually sought to be caught, because working two weeks for Stevenson-Hamilton was far less onerous than paying for the Portuguese permit.

Stevenson-Hamilton recognized the road building as a key to the success of the park. He wrote: "In 1928, 122 miles of road had been completed; in 1929, 382; in 1930, 450; and by 1936 approximately 900. The tourist traffic rose in like proportion from three cars with a dozen visitors in 1927, to over 6,000 cars and lorries, carrying about 26,000 in 1935."[62]

Today the tourist traffic far exceeds one million people each year, much of it following roadbeds laid down by the Mozambican labor.

Thus did Stevenson-Hamilton seek to balance all things.

He had established an ecology of nature by saving the lions. He had established an economic and social ecology as well by funding the park with tourist dollars. The deal with the immigrants and the roads they built redoubled his efforts and set in motion a productive cycle. The Shangan Mozambicans built more roads; more tourists came; more lions were protected by more rangers, financed by more tourists who used the new roads to see the increasing numbers of lions, which required more roads and more Mozambicans.

The key part, the major paradigm shift, was that the visitors now underwrote the park. The political sway of hunters and ranchers was over. The future of the park now lay with those who wanted to save the lions, not exterminate them.

The "lion war" of the first part of the twentieth century had been won. Threatened as a species, lions thrived in Kruger National Park. The tourists had saved them.

Or, if you viewed it another way, the lions had saved Kruger National Park by assuring a steady stream of tourist traffic to fund its upkeep.

Whichever way you viewed it, the relationship between humans and lions had changed. Perhaps it was not clear at the time, but there it was just the same.

Just as there was a new breed of ranger in the park, now there was a corollary: a new breed of lion that had no reason to fear humans. And in addition to those two new breeds was a third—the first greens. These were tourists who were captivated by nature and adored the wild and would protect it vigorously. Each group and both species depended on one another.

The change at Kruger and other parks or preserves throughout Africa about this time was of immense significance in the relationship of the two species. Because we live in the context of a newer paradigm, it is hard to appreciate how radical a change that was.

In *The Iliad* by Homer, Achilles addressed his adversary, Hector, famously and proclaimed that there "can be no covenant between men and lions." But of course in a larger sense there always had been. The covenant was that once we were lion food. Then we were rivals, competitive alpha predators, vying for the top rank on the food chain, circling each other warily over kills, killing the other when the chance presented itself, much as hyenas and lions do now.

Only in this most recent era did humans decide to make lions their buddies. Only in the last half century or so did humans feel safe enough to indulge themselves in exploring the more mystical and spiritual connections to their former carnivorous competitors.

And place all cynicism aside. There *is* a mystical and spiritual connection. Among green champions, the rangers, the tourists, the guides, hunters, the scientists, anyone who has spent time near lions in the wild, there *is* something between humans and lions, some special bond or understanding, some unnamed, unspoken covenant that all feel when they encounter lions in the wild.

There is the "look" tourists have. It seems akin to the hypnotic state brought forth by the embers of a campfire. In both, humans seem to seek a timeless connection. There is a communion, a wordless memory of prehistoric nights. It struggles to be heard as the seekers stare through the fire, through the lion, through a portal to an ancient and ageless understanding that nearly can be, but never quite is, spoken.

Even the experts struggle with the concept. The famed field biologist and lion man George Schaller theorized that the contact of early man to animals was more with early lion than early ape. Lions lived in prides and hunted, often in a coordinated and cooperative manner, just as early man lived in tribes and hunted in teams. Genetically, we might have descended from apes; ecologically and socially, we evolved more from interaction with lions. A study of lions, Schaller suggested, "mirrors man as much as any of the recent ones about monkeys or apes, and mankind can learn more about itself and the evolution of its social systems through lions . . . than by examining some vegetarian monkey."[63]

So perhaps we see lions as teachers. Or as competitors with which to match wits. Hans Kruuk agrees, in a manner of speaking. He notes that in the wild predators and prey alike study the big predators and seem at times transfixed by them. He too attributes this to a natural impulse to learn from a threat, from a rival.

Veteran park zoologist G. L. Smuts could speak only of "'the sensation' I and others experience when we are in close proximity to lions."[64] Randall Eaton, a South African scientist, once noted that "(t)he lion is us. . . . We need wilderness in our world to expand our awareness and tame our lion hearts."[65]

Choose your explanation for the new covenant: scientific, economic, spiritual, or just plain recreational. The new covenant not only worked, it produced prosperity and satisfaction for the rangers, the tourists, and the lions and, for several years, the Mozambicans.

The view would change substantially for Mozambicans, however. They viewed lions with awe and respect, and for a while the park and its lions were an economic boon to be certain, but there would come a time in the 1960s when they would be bound by a different covenant altogether.

For tens of thousands of years, lions and humans were copredators, facing off over their respective kills. But the Mozambican immigrants would reach a state where they were no longer bush-smart workers, but weak, defenseless refugees from war and poverty, drought, famine, and pestilence. The Mozambicans would no longer be dominant over lions or even copredators with lions.

Their new covenant with lions would be this: the Mozambican refugees would become purely and simply meat. They would be transformed into a prey species.

Chapter 5

THE NEW REFUGEES

The forces that have drawn Mozambicans to South Africa for a century and more are revealed; the case of brave John Khoza; his terrible plight and fantastic flight; how refugees were forced by apartheid to travel at night; the terrible wars and plagues and famines and droughts that have increased the refugees' numbers; park lions, no longer fearful of humans, treat the trek of refugees as a great migration of easy prey.

Tell the tales of the friendship and the bonds of the bush, Neville had said, and I can tell he and Steve have forged bonds everywhere we stop. We are traveling back through the south of the park, spotting game as casually as a motorist might spot sparrows in the suburbs, when we drive over the Crocodile River and leave the park.

My request to find and interview a Mozambican refugee leads us to Izinyoni Lodge in Marloth Park, a community just south of Kruger. Neville and Steve are greeted as family by Paddy Buckmaster, the owner of the lodge; Pauline, his wife; and John Khoza and his beautiful young daughter, Coley.

"Oh, Neville, and how *are* you doing with your cobras?" Pauline says. "Has he told the cobra stories, the stories about the spitting cobras? He runs into them *everywhere*."

As has she, truth be told. A few years ago, she walked into the laundry room and saw a Mozambican spitting cobra coiled in the corner. The cobras can spit venom into the eyes of predators and prey, blinding them for short periods, or permanently if cold water and medical care are not administered quickly. The venom travels with the velocity of water from a squirt gun. The cobra nailed Pauline squarely in the eyes before she quite knew it was there.

It beat a hasty retreat and she stumbled toward the lavatory and washed out the venom before calling for help. She received immediate medical care, but still she was blinded for a bit and recovered her full vision only gradually over a period of days.

Because of its ability to project venom so accurately, some rank the spitting cobra as among the most dangerous snake in the park. And here again, of course, incidents with deadly snakes are not without their history in Kruger, or examples of what it feels like to be spat at in the eyes by a cobra.

"At M't timba, one day, I was leaning over the edge of the table in order to pick up something," Wolhuter wrote long ago, "when suddenly it seemed as if two red-hot needles had pierced my eyes."

It was, of course, a spitting cobra, and Wolhuter's eyes remained very painful, despite immediate treatment, "and I was quite blind for three days and had to remain in a dark room, but gradually, to my unbounded relief, my eyes recovered completely."[66]

Yet it was not Wolhuter who had the truly serious problems with snakes but his beloved dogs who traveled with him everywhere. And his problems were not with cobras but with the most feared snake in the park, hands down: the black mamba.

The mamba is feared both for real reasons and a host of fables. It is said to be able to travel faster than a running man, even a horse. That is an exaggeration, but scientists confirm that the snake can reach speeds of ten miles per hour—not a leisurely stroll and fast enough to catch many humans if for some unlikely reason it wanted to.

Mambas can grow nearly fourteen feet long and when disturbed, they may rise up three to four feet off the ground, and can travel in that mode as well. Their aggressiveness and the deadliness of mamba venom is not contested. Few animals survive a bite without quick medical attention.[67]

Harry Wolhuter discovered this to his great sorrow once while patrolling with a pack of his favorite dogs. Wolhuter was a great lover of dogs even before one saved him from the lion, and in the wild they gave him expanded senses. They could hear and smell animals far before he could.

So it was that one day this pack closed on a black mamba before Wolhuter came within gun range. The big snake took them down, one after the other. By the time Wolhuter reached the scene, one of his dogs was already dead, a few wobbling as the toxin paralyzed their systems, and a few others still attacked and were bitten again and again by the mamba. There was little he could do. Once bitten, they were dead dogs walking, so to speak, and all seven died right there.

The largest snake in the park, the python, is less dangerous to man and nonvenomous. Still, one took a toll on Wolhuter's dogs. In a scene similar to the mamba incident, Wolhuter's pack once cornered a large python. Wolhuter reached the scene and shooed them away from the snake, which he meant no harm. Then he counted his dogs. One of them, a feisty fox terrier, was missing.

When he called and the dog did not come, Wolhuter looked at the nearby python and noticed a terrier-sized bulge midway down the snake's throat. A sentimentalist when it came to dogs but not snakes, Wolhuter dispatched the python so he could bury his little terrier. He sliced the snake open at the bulge, and the terrier fell limply onto the ground, slimy with digestive juices and blood, motionless, as still as roadkill.

Then it took a deep breath, stood up, shook its head and body, and rejoined the pack as if nothing much had happened.[68]

In the context of such stories, the small crowd at Izinyoni urge Neville on to tell his famous cobra stories. Steve stays in the background but wears a particularly devilish look on his face. He knows Edwards does not want to tell these stories.

"Later?" Neville says simply, but everyone insists, and he relents.

His was even a hairier tale than Pauline's or even Wolhuter's, though it took place in civilization and not in the bush.

He was on a ladder painting his home and lodge in the days when he was still married, with a brush in one hand and solvent-soaked cloth in the other. He had not noticed the cobra in the tree, and the cobra had not noticed him. When it did, the snake nailed him in both eyes, which was bad enough, but what Neville did next made matters far worse. He reflexively mopped his eyes with the rag soaked in a strong solvent. Now he was blinded both by the venom and the paint solvent. He required hospital care. For a while, it was touch and go whether he would see again.

But we get only the one cobra story with the promise of others later. We are after all searching for Mozambican refugees who have made it across Kruger and established new lives in South Africa. The goal here is to understand what drives them across the fence, past the rangers and army patrols, and into the fiercer threat of the lions. Steve and Neville know of one man who faced all those threats more than once.

In fact, we do not have to go far to meet him. John Khoza, Paddy Buckmaster's right-hand man and de facto younger brother, is the refugee. He is settled in South Africa now, but how he got there was no small accomplishment.

His ancestors would have had an easier time of it. The threat of the lions is relatively new—a product of the second half of the twentieth century. For decades, the flow of Mozambicans through Kruger National Park was a given, and there were no problems with the lions. The human treks were as regular a part of nature as the migration of wildebeests or zebras during dry seasons. There was an irresistible draw from the ever-so-strong South African mining and farming economies. An economic osmosis pulled Mozambicans through the thin membrane of Kruger and into the mines and ranches. So integral to the culture was the crossing of the park that it became a rite of passage, a sign of manhood among Mozambican youths. "Jompe joz," they would call it when they jumped the border.[69] Or they would tell friends they were "goin' west to Jonni"—to Johannesburg—and nearly every young man would make the trip if he were to be thought of as a man.

What changed an arduous but uneventful commute into a life-threatening trek was a force that would reshape South Africa for decades. A nationalist movement among the Afrikaners swept the nation in 1948 and soon wrote racist distinctions into law. Apartheid changed everything in Kruger. The once-common migration of black Africans across South African borders, active for nearly a century, was discouraged. By the 1960s, when Mozambicans revolted against the Portuguese colonial government, larger numbers of Mozambicans sought refuge in South Africa. The borders between the park and Mozambique gradually were fenced off. Then areas of the fence were electrified with lethal voltage and the border patrolled.

There is no consensus that this stopped the flow of immigrants or even slowed it much—though nearly a hundred refugees are said to have died on the wires.[70] The demand for their labor was still strong; their need to work in South Africa was as acute. Many of the mine owners and operators and ranchers winked at the law, and the immigrants hardly blinked at the new barriers. The closing of the border worked about as well as the U.S.-Mexican effort—which is to say, not well.

What changed was the manner in which Mozambicans traveled. Patrols and helicopters would spot them in the daytime. So the Mozambicans began traveling only at night, when they were harder to see and most of the guards and rangers were asleep.

The lions, of course, were very much awake, and in fact preferred to hunt at night. Thus was a new confrontation formed. The Mozambican migration might have been an irresistible force, but it was about to meet an immovable carnivore—an African lion that had no fear of human beings.

Still, they kept coming. Years later an ardent anti-immigration government official threw up his hands in frustration. "Lions do not stop them, hippos do not stop them, crocodiles do not stop them, nothing can stop them."

To understand fully why that is so, it is best to meet an irresistible force in person.

Even as a young boy, John Khoza had a bearing of goodwill and intelligence. Big brown eyes peered out from beneath an inquisitive brow. He seemed to be forever questioning his situation, looking for the right, good choice among options that mostly were bad. Perhaps hidden in that demeanor, or just below its surface, was the other thing, the intense drive and determination that would send him on his path in life. One might call it will, or even willfulness at special moments.

During my visit, John sat on a rock slightly above us as he told his story. The flat raking light of early evening and a setting sun cast long shadows and imparted a golden texture to the air, the plants, the buildings, the river, and, just beyond the river, the trees in the park. I could see cape buffalo in the park less than three hundred feet away, and John would gesture north toward the river and the park and east toward Mozambique as he told his story. Neville and Steve squatted on the ground nearby, jumping in to translate when John's English failed him or my questions needed elaboration.

He was among the first of the modern surge of refugees through Kruger back in the 1970s. As always, they were pulled there by the South African economy. They were pushed there by the poverty of Mozambique. South Africa, they would say, was the America of Africa.

What pulled many Mozambicans through the park too was family and tribal kinships. Decades ago, when the park was formed, many of the Shangan tribe, about three thousand, were expelled— literally driven from Eden. Some went east to Mozambique, and some went west to Mpumalanga Province in South Africa, just west of Kruger. The Shangans called Stevenson-Hamilton "Skukuza"—the one who turns things upside down. For the white conservationist, the nickname was a compliment. He had turned slaughter into salvation and he proudly named the headquarters camp Skukuza. For the indigenous, the nickname described what he had done to their lives. By the mid-twentieth century, if one was Shangan and traveled over the river and through the woods to see family, Kruger was the woods and the Crocodile was the river. It was natural for families to get together. Kruger was the commute.

There were few recorded notices of dustups with the lions before apartheid. Yes, Africans and Europeans alike occasionally ended up inside a lion. But it was not systematic. The one ominous exception was at the outbreak of the Boer War in 1898. The mines shut down for a period, and the Mozambican workers were simply given the boot. They made a forced march through Kruger, with many sick and unfit to travel. The lions soon began picking them off—and then a British sentry or two as well.

Stevenson-Hamilton noted this in his log. He thought the phenomenon easily explained. Lions and all other carnivores take easy prey first. The long columns of sick and dying workers had taught the cats that the refugees were there for the taking, and the habit expanded to the occasional Englishman on lonely guard duty.[71]

Similar conditions were brewing in 1972, but with a number of important differences that would move the man-eater meter considerably. By the 1970s, the refugees were not just seeking work, they were fleeing a war with the Portuguese colonial government.

Moreover, so frequent were natural catastrophes in Mozambique that the word *catastrophe*, with its implication of rare occurrence, did not seem appropriate. With great regularity, Mozambique cycled through famine and flood. For months, sometimes a year, no rain would fall. Corn would wither. Cattle would die. Then, when the rains came, they would come too hard and too fast. They would sweep away fields, herds, villages, people, and the very soil that only yesterday had been so dry it blew in the wind. Locusts too might suddenly ruin a good year.

And these catastrophes, which came almost like seasons in Mozambique, would pulse swarms of refugees across the park into South Africa.

Times had changed for the lions of Kruger as well, of course. Wolhuter had noted the phenomenon in the 1920s. Even after his run-in, he had been accustomed to riding out into the park with nothing more than a fly swatter to keep the insects at bay. But after he saw lions stalking him, he revised that casual approach and always carried a rifle. Once he tested his theory that the lions were actually after his horse and not him. He dismounted, expecting the lion to run for the hills. But the lioness kept coming, stalking Wolhuter on foot, until he fired his rifle.

The lions were no longer fearful of man. A generation or two of lions had grown up in the park knowing mankind as a passive, even benevolent, force. Men and women rode in cars and gaped at antelope, warthogs, rhinos, and lions in the daytime. In their cars, the people were safe and seen by the lions as harmless. But a man on horseback or on foot could prompt a different reaction. The association with large spear-bearing hunting parties or white men with guns was lost to the protected lions. In fact, the men who carried dangerous weapons mostly protected the lions from poachers. True, poachers took their toll. Cruel snare traps did as well. Bovine tuberculosis infected hundreds of lions in the park. But the worst experience for most lions with humans in the 1970s was to hear the pop of a dart gun, stumble drunkenly, and then wake up with a hangover, a dose of antibiotics, and a tracking collar.

So these were the conditions John Khoza faced in 1972 at the age of fifteen.

He was from a good family in a small Mozambique village, and his father owned many cattle. John was smart. And he was a favored child. He was the pride of his young mother.

Disease—John does not know which—claimed his mother when he was ten. The loss hurt, of course, but his will or willfulness offset the loss. He resolved to be educated on his own and began attending school on his own. His father, well-to-do, encouraged him. Others would watch the herd.

Then disease—John does not know which—killed his father and orphaned him at fifteen. John and his older brother would have been affluent by Mozambique standards and American law, but in Mozambique the cattle passed to his uncle, and of all John's adoring relatives his uncle was not among them. His uncle saw John and his brother as rivals to the herd. John had to drop out from school. All day, he was forced to work, and at night there would be only a bowl of mealies, of corn. Then famine struck Mozambique, and the bowl of mealies became haphazard. He was malnourished, without a future. His uncle was starving him out of any claim to the herd, and there was no other food or job to be had. That is when he and two friends decided to do it, to take the only option they had: to cross the Kruger. *Jompe joz.* At fifteen, it was time to be a man.

There are three strategies for crossing Kruger and two professions that have grown up around the crossings. The first strategy is no strategy at all. Just walk west at night. This is the simplest form of "going west to Jonni." Often, it ends badly.

The second is to obtain *muti*, magic from the local traditional healer. Often this is a totem, like a hyena's tail, guaranteed to repel lions, though it is difficult for consumers to collect on the warranty when one malfunctions. ("The hyena's tail?" says one ranger. "Yes, it works very well on humans and keeps humans away. Not so well on lions.") Still, the market for muti is good.

The third strategy, and by far the most effective, is to hire a guide. Passports and visas at the border cost around $50—a tough sell on an annual income of $300. A guide can be had for less. Often, he will take twenty to thirty across at great profit, and even then there are no guarantees. "If you become sick, if you are carrying a baby, if you are old and cannot keep up?" said a ranger who knows this technique.

"Then you are likely to be left behind. The guide cannot take a chance."[72]

John was lucky to know a guide named Fredie. Luckier still to know lions. He had herded, and herders must of need come into contact with lions. He knew, most important, what not to do, but Fredie told them anyway. "You must not run from a lion. If you run, the lion will kill you."

So, at 2 A.M. on a dark July night in 1972, when the migration already was under way, John and his small party found where a warthog had burrowed under the fence. They wriggled under and set out across the very southern end of the park. At night, they could see the lights of towns beyond the park to their left. That was their low-tech compass and GPS. By day, they found a shady tree in a remote part of the bush. There they talked and slept.

"You do not take food, you do not worry about water," John said. "You do not take clothes or worry about what you will wear. You are starving. You move with purpose through the bush. You move with purpose. You stay off the roads and away from the helicopters, the rangers on bicycles, the army patrols, and the tourists."

They would see elephants, and move cautiously. They encountered cape buffalo and one night—ever the herdsmen—threw rocks at the dangerous animals to move them on. And then, the second night, the lions found them. Said John: "I stopped. I froze. We all did. I faced the lion in front of me. But I knew too there were at least two or three to the rear. Always, there are lions to the rear. We stopped. We waited. We did not move. We were absolutely still. Ten minutes passed. Fifteen minutes passed. Then we did not count the time."

Eventually, seeing no obvious vulnerabilities, seeing no trigger signs, the lions moved on to easier, surer prey. It was the "stand" rangers and zoologists speak of so often. Make a stand against a lion, remaining motionless, and as often as not the lion will eventually move on. And for John it worked.

It was a scene and a process repeated again and again, many times a night when they were in the park. But always, the former herdsmen knew to make the stand firm and true, giving no sign of vulnerability, no attack trigger.

And eventually, they made it to the Crocodile River, swam that appropriately named body of water, survived it, and were free in South Africa.

John Khoza found good work on a farm. By South African standards, he was at the bottom of the barrel. By Khoza standards he was on top of the world. Perhaps he was at the bottom of the barrel, but at least he was not at the bottom of the food chain.

He had food to eat. He had a job.

He was in short a happy man. By Mozambique standards, he was blessed. He was blessed until the day, many years after his crossing, in 1985, that a uniformed man stopped him as he walked, picked him out, John does not know how, and asked him for his papers.

John had none. The man put him in a truck. The truck drove him through Kruger to the Mozambique border. He was placed in a holding area with dozens of other men. They were all going back, back to Mozambique, where the droughts, floods, civil war, and starvation were killing even more people in the 1980s than they had in the 1970s.

John milled around in the crowd and then inspected the perimeter of the fence. There was nothing out there, only the bush. The authorities did not need a heavy fence. They did not need to charge it with electricity. No one would jump the fence and run toward the lions of Kruger.

John looked at the fence. He looked at the guards.

Then he was through the fence and running through Kruger. He was running for his life.

What made John run was fear of returning to a Mozambique that was far, far worse even than the one he had left in 1972.

What made the prospect of returning to Mozambique induce such fear was a confluence of every pestilence known to man short of earthquake and volcanic eruption. Political, economic, and meteorological curses had all aligned in one devastating front and swept the country for years.

There was not one flood, not one drought, not one brief war, but year upon year of them all. The drought and flood cycles continued on what seemed an increased frequency. Locusts at one point literally descended upon the agrarian country. Pure water was scarce. Malaria and mosquito control were nonexistent.

But perhaps worst of all was the human-wrought pestilence.

The Mozambique liberation movement—the Frelimo (Mozambican Liberation Front)—won its independence from a brutal Portuguese colonial government in 1974 after eleven years of fighting. Overnight, it seemed, the vast majority of Portuguese farmers, industrialists, and merchants packed their bags and their capital and left.[73]

"They did not leave a light bulb," one writer said of the exodus.

The economy had not completely imploded when Frelimo established a Marxist government. It joined the boycott of apartheid South Africa and Rhodesia, and, it was said, funded antiapartheid guerilla movements in those countries. Those still very powerful states in turn helped finance an anti-Marxist guerilla force within Mozambique called Renamo (Mozambican National Resistance).

Frelimo and Renamo fought, and in the fighting both sides "impressed" Mozambican men into service. Renamo, particularly, was known for annihilating villages that were reluctant to send men. Family structures were fractured, tribes and villages dispersed or destroyed.

The U.S. State Department, not known for its opposition to those fighting Marxist governments, officially pronounced in 1988 that Renamo had perpetrated "one of the most brutal holocausts against ordinary human beings since World War II."[74]

The unofficial words were far more telling. They came from the refugees and soldiers, talking to relief workers:[75]

Said Augustin, a refugee: "One night we heard a loud knock on the door. We didn't open it, so it was kicked in. Bandits, Renamo soldiers, burst in. They used the bayonets attached to their guns to stab my mother, father and brother. I ran into the bush where I hid until the next day. When I returned, I found that my parents and my brother were dead and that the bandits burned our house down."

Said a drafted thirteen-year-old Renamo soldier: "We went into the house where a woman was there with her baby. The bandits [Renamo] gave her a knife and ordered her to kill her baby. She refused and the bandits screamed and screamed at her. Finally, she stabbed the child. . . . While we were returning to the base, the bandits got angry at captives who couldn't keep up. Some of the bandits took axes and killed those who couldn't continue. They chopped off arms or legs and cut up the rest of their bodies until they were dead."

Said an eleven-year-old boy from Sofala: "The bandits came to our house and told my mother to give them food. My mother told them we didn't have any. They beat her until she died. All this time, they were holding my father back. They left and took my father with them. He didn't come back. . . . I think they killed him.

"I was alone with my younger sister and four brothers. I couldn't get other people to help us get food because nobody had any. I began to go into the bush and search for roots that I brought back to feed my sister and brothers. I had to keep going farther and farther into the bush to find enough roots. While I was away, my sister died. Then my brothers began to die one by one. Then my last brother died. I left that night. I walked for two days and two nights until I was safe."

Famine was upon the land. Land mines were everywhere. Massacres of every inhabitant of villages were common. People died, first by the hundreds, then by the thousands, then by the tens of thousands, and finally by the hundreds of thousands. Mozambique by any measure became one of the poorest nations on the globe; per capita income was less than $300 a year.

The results were inevitable. Thousands of refugees turned west to South Africa and to Kruger. No longer were they pulled by the South African economy. The famine and the persecution pushed them.

They crossed fields of land mines, but did not stop. They came to a lethally charged fence, but did not stop. They came to Kruger and knew the lions were there, but did not think about stopping.

"When you are starving," Neville said one day as we looked out across the Crocodile River at Kruger, "the lions and the park are an acceptable risk."

And of course, the converse is true. When you are a lion and you see weak, starving people stumbling and dying in front of you, there is no risk. There is only easy prey.

Thousands crossed the park each year in the 1970s, but in the 1980s and 1990s the traffic was ratcheted up by the war, the plagues, the floods, the droughts, the famines. The capture rate of Mozambicans in the park in 1982 was about two thousand a year. By 1985 the capture rate was fifteen hundred a month—about eighteen thousand for the year. The actual traffic through the park was immensely larger. A map created by the U.S. Committee for Refugees in 1986 shows a broad arrow running from Mozambique directly through Kruger, labeled "160,000–220,000."[76] This is likely a conservative number. The total number of Mozambique refugees—those literally driven from the country—was about forty-five thousand in 1984. It rose to nearly two hundred twenty thousand in 1985, to three hundred fifty thousand in 1986, and to more than nine hundred thousand in the plague year of 1987.

By 1990 it had increased by another half million and by 1993, the total number of refugees—many of them passing directly through Kruger—stood at 1.7 million.[77]

It was a great migration of mammals, not unlike the seasonal movements of wildebeests. And in Africa, whenever there is a great migration of mammals, there is also a great convocation of carnivores—a predators' ball. They gather to pick off the weak, the lame, the old, and the sick. The prey species can be wildebeests. Or Mozambicans. The carnivores do not care.

"Exactly," said Gerrie Camacho, a zoologist and chief scientist of the Mpumalanga Parks Board in Nelspruit, who has studied lions all his adult life.

"Exactly," said Willelm Gertenbach, the head of conservation for Kruger, in a separate interview some days later.

If caught in South Africa, any Mozambican was immediately deported back into the maelstrom of Mozambique, only to join the mass migration of the starving, wounded, old, and poor, moving first across territory larded with hundreds of thousands of land mines, and then back into Kruger, where they faced the lions.

And so John ran.

He was at the edge of the camp, and at first he thought no one had seen him. Then he heard footsteps close behind. When he turned, he saw only two other refugees. "Take us with you," one gasped, and what was he to do? Take them back instead?

The three ran through the bush. Antelope scattered. No lions. Zebras snorted and then bolted. No lions. John feared running over a pride of lions in his haste. Antelope occasionally do that. The dozing lions instantly switch on and sometimes catch antelope in midleap. It is the trigger point mentioned by rangers—a reflex so fast it seems to fire from the muscle itself, not the eye and brain.

The men ran, then hid. John was certain someone would be following. He could not wait until dark. He ran again and bore left. He must get across the Crocodile River, he thought. He must get across and then lose himself in the agricultural workers of South Africa, in the great farms and workforces walking the roads each day to the fields, in the diaspora of refugees.

And then he was there, on the banks of the Crocodile. He had arrived suddenly, from over a rise, and of need drew up sharply to avoid entering the river. He could hear the slap and splash of crocodiles entering the water—entering their river. He looked back, saw the two other refugees and said, "We must swim."

The two men recoiled in horror. "I cannot swim!" one said. "Wait until dark and then come back with a rope and pull us across."

"No! We must cross now!" John said. "We will be caught! Swim!"

And with that, he dove into the water and swam furiously. The Crocodile River was about one hundred feet wide at the crossing, and John just looked straight ahead and drove directly through the water in a frantic crawl. If the crocs got him, they got him. He could do nothing about it. He could do nothing more about that than he could about the two refugees back on the bank. He could only take the choice he had in front of him. If he made it? And found a rope? Perhaps, but now only the far bank was on his mind.

Nothing stopped him. Nothing pulled him under. He made the far bank, lifted himself up, and did not turn to encourage the other two. He made for the road and for the fields. He was moving with force and purpose.

He reached the road just outside Kruger Park and looked for any other workers. He needed to blend in quickly. Around a near curve came an armored Land Rover moving fast. It moved faster when the policemen inside saw John, and before he could run again he was looking at the muzzle of an R5 South African assault rifle.

"What are you doing?" the officer with the rifle said. "Where are your papers?"

John was dripping wet and not far from the water. He had fallen into the river and lost his papers, he told the policemen. One barked a laugh and the other grabbed John and frog-marched him at gunpoint to the Land Rover. They put him in the backseat and told him to stay there. One radioed in their capture while another smoked and looked out over the river dreamily into Kruger.

John looked at Kruger on one side and at the fields of maize, of mealies, on the other. He had been so close.

Was still close, actually, if you looked at it in a different way. If you figured the odds and took a calculated gamble. The fields were just a hundred feet or so away. He looked at the door of the Land Rover. It was not locked. One man was on the radio. The one with the rifle still looked toward the Kruger landscape, smoking.

John flung open the door and bolted. He ran for the cornfields. He looked directly ahead. This was like swimming the Croc. If it happened, it happened. If they shot, they shot.

He heard a shout. No shots. He heard the rhythms of their sturdy boots running after him. Still no shots.

Then he was in the corn, the maize, through the mealies, away from the white officers who pursued him. He ran through the standing corn, out into a clearing, into a large stand of corn again, and into a long, cleared corridor of stubble. He turned once and saw them behind him. They were long-legged, large, young white men, and they were gaining on him. John was short, just five foot four. He could hear their heavy boots clopping hard on the cultivated ground.

Ahead of him, he could see workers. They dropped their tools and turned toward the chase. He rounded a bend in the field and the cleared portion and for a moment the pursuing officers dropped from view. The field workers became animated. They were motioning to him. They were Mozambican. "Go here, friend!" one said and pointed toward the standing corn. "Go here!"

John juked to the left and ran through the standing corn. He was short. The corn was tall. He was invisible after traveling thirty feet. In the clearing, the white men turned the bend and faced two cleared paths through the field. The workers pointed toward the right-hand bend, and the white men followed the fingers, running down a curving route that never gave them a clear field of vision. They ran right past where John stood motionless, hidden from view.

John walked through the field of corn and into the vastness of the great South African veld and was free again. There was no chance to help those two back at the river. It did not work that way. They knew the rules. They had to fend for themselves.

He worked construction for a while and then ran into Paddy Buckmaster and helped him build his lodge on the banks of the

Crocodile right on a sweeping curve of the river that exposed a fantastic tableau of Kruger, water buffalo, and sometimes lions and crocs as well.

The two men became close, and Paddy would say to John, "Listen, John, I know you are Mozambican. There are things we can do for you for citizenship."

Even with Paddy, John was steadfast. That willfulness of his. "No," he said, "I am South African."

Even after apartheid fell, John declined Paddy's help. Then one day, a local policeman, a holdover bully from the days of apartheid who had no love for Paddy or John, detained John and scheduled him for deportation.

An infuriated Paddy Buckmaster and his attorney showed up, and Buckmaster demanded, "What the bloody hell do you think you are doing to that man? He has worked for me for fifteen years."

The attorney attacked as a Doberman might, and the policeman backed off quickly. Paddy and the attorney were able to establish permanent citizenship for John. He has a wife and six children now and drives a spotless four-wheel-drive truck.

"John?" Neville says simply. "You've done well."

chapter 6

THE RULES OF LIONS, THE RULES OF MAZ

I make a proposal; the habits of successful man-eaters are reviewed; tigers and lions are compared by two experts; I face some choices; how lions behave and are attracted to human prey; the modern myths of lions and humans revealed; we meet a modern Wolhuter; his brave battle on behalf of lions; his individual struggle with a specific lion.

The warden of Marloth Park, the community just south of Kruger across the Crocodile River where Izinyoni is located, drops by Paddy's lodge to chat with Neville, Steve, and me. He has guided lion hunters and still does, but ducks his head slightly when he says it. "I'd rather not, but the hunters pay the rent, you see, for the conservation and all."

The spookiest he has ever felt, he says, was once when tracking a lion with a client. The tracks were fresh and clear. The men moved in a wide circle, and then they came back upon their own boot prints—overprinted by the pug marks of a large lion. The lion the men were tracking had turned the tables, circled behind them, and was tracking them.

"We never saw him," the warden says.[78] Steve and Neville nod in agreement, indicating they have been in similar situations. "But I tell you at that moment, every piece of me was alive and looking for anything that moved in the bush," the warden said.

Everything moved, of course, except the lion. The men left empty-handed, glad to be alive.

We talk more with John Khoza. His seems an incredible story. But the incredible part is that it is not uncommon at all. It is repeated thousands of times each year, sometimes with happy endings, many times not. John is an Everyman of the immigrants. Nothing will stop Mozambicans from migrating through Kruger to South Africa. They are the irresistible force.

To understand the immovable object—the lions—my safari follows the literal tracks of lions but also a paper trail along the path of what is known about man-eating lions, or—a nuanced but important distinction—lions that may happen to eat a man.

In modern Kruger, tourists and game rangers alike avoid testing the lion's skill at attacking humans by applying well what they know about the animal's nastier habits.

"When you get into trouble with a lion?" Neville says with the inevitable inflection of a question. "You may find that it is very hard to get out of trouble? So the best thing to do? What you really should consider first? Knowing enough not to get into trouble to begin with."

First and foremost, they say, avoid the night. It is at night, of course, that the refugees follow the paths we follow now. And it is at night that the lions hunt. Tourists leave the park or retreat to the barbed-wire-encircled compounds and campgrounds, and are allowed out only in daylight. However, lions will kill in the daytime. They are opportunistic, and if a meal drops into their laps—a man falling from a horse into a lion's mouth, to choose Wolhuter's unlucky example—lions will dine at high noon. Typically, though, the serious hunting is done at night.

It was at about this point, I know not exactly when, that it seemed particularly important for me to be there, in the night, when the serious hunting is done. How else could a journalist get it right? How else could proper witness be borne? I had to walk Kruger.

So it was that I came to inquire of Neville and Steve what I would need to cross the park at night. What would they recommend, if I were to mount a night expedition on foot? What would it take?

"I'm a professional hunter," Steve Gibson said. "I am not a professional fool."

Neville Edwards, ever the diplomat, nevertheless uttered an obscenity. It was the only curse word I heard from him during the entire safari.

"If you are talking about walking the Kruger at night, you are asking for real shit!" His face had turned slightly red, but I didn't take the hint and pressed on. It was my risk, after all. What would you do? How would you do it? Would we just sneak in? How would we do it? Theoretically?

"*Theoretically*, if we could get permission? I would put you and me in the middle, and we would have rifles? I would have four rangers on the points of the compass out from us twenty feet armed with shotguns? We would be certain to run into lion, and something or someone would be certain to die.

"On those terms, would that be something you really would want to do?"

I made a meaningless mumble that neither confirmed nor denied what I would like to do. Truth was, I had not thought of the ramifications, save to myself. Clearly I had violated the Steve-Neville code of the bush. Other codes as well. Edwards has a duty to protect his clients, to keep them from harm. It wasn't going to be him and me just sneaking under a fence from bush to bush, playing kick the can with some big kitties. Ethically, he could not expose me to that risk and keep his license. He would have to go in armed and at near platoon strength. More than that, I had violated the Steve-Neville code of the bush in another way: proposing a foolhardy gambit without considering consequences that could cause serious and senseless harm, not just to me but to animals and rangers, too. You could swim in croc-infested lakes and pools if you had scoped it out and had a chance. You could not take on a project that was bound to lead to tragedy for someone.

But the trickier part was that my journalist's instinct—the one with the devil's pitchfork instead of the halo, the one that is despicable but some days undeniably useful—also made me think that I might get Neville to do it, or some version of it. He had not said no, just posed the ethical question: would I still want to do it?

Well, yeah. Part of me did. But the thought had been for me to put my head in the lion's mouth, so to speak, not to literally endanger rangers—or lions. I had to think about that now, carefully.

I had gone over this ground generally with my friend Tom Masland—Maz we often called him. He had been in and out of nearly every war in Africa for the last nine years and nearly every war and riot in the Middle East for ten years before that. In all that time, he had taken just three frags from a rocket propelled grenade (RPG) "A cheap purple heart," was his typical laconic comment. He had a deceptively laid-back manner to him. His cool masked the shrewd analyst he was both of politics, people, and place. He knew how to get around. He would always go for the story and he always would come back with it. I knew that at least two veteran Reuters correspondents had died in another conflict he had covered, and I wanted to know how he had sorted it all out, survived to cover another war, picked the smoking hot RPG shards out of his arm and laughed it off, when the others had died.

It was a true mystery to me. In the States, I knew my way around tough spots well enough. I'd been through riots, police-gang gunfights, was roughed up a bit by police when I attempted to reach demonstrations, and then manually thrown out of meetings of the militant groups that were demonstrating. It was all part of the game as a journalist.

On one memorable evening in Philadelphia, during a small but quite serious riot in 1980, I found myself well past police lines talking to a mother and her four children, all of descending age and size. All of us were huddled in a doorway. Then Molatovs and pistol shots started coming from the rioters to the north; police shotgun blasts and tear gas grenades were the answering fire from the south. We shrank into the doorway, could hear the whine of the incoming slugs, feel the police shotgun wadding raining down on the street in front of us, smell the cordite and the whiffs of tear gas drifting back toward us. The Molatovs were not reaching the police or even exploding, but they were walking in perilously close to us, and the street smelled of gas.

"Are you the press?" the mother asked me, and I said that was me. "Then you can get us out of here," she said.

She then promptly pushed me up out of the doorway. With press credentials held high, I then lead a conga line, the family crouched behind me in descending age and size, right through no-man's land. She kept yelling, "We the press, baby! Don't nobody shoot." And no one did.

But that was in North Philly, tough, but not Africa tough. A stunt like that can get you killed easily in a land where dead-eyed twelve-year-olds wield automatic weapons. I needed the rules according to Tom Masland. I needed the Rules of Maz.

The Rules of Maz were this. You got the story. You wrote it right—true and authentic. The rule I didn't know was deceptively simple. Every foreign correspondent in a war zone has a local "fixer," someone on the ground in-country who knows the culture and the community. You only moved where you knew what was likely to happen. You made sure you had good fixers, and then you listened to them. Correspondents who have good fixers and listen to them live; those who don't, or don't listen, tend to die. The Reuters guys were told by their fixers not to drive any farther; the reporters didn't trust the fixers, dropped them off, drove on, and died.

And there was the rub—a conflict of rules. You had to find good fixers and then follow them. But you also had to get the story. And you had to have a good fix on how good your fixers were.

I knew I had good guides—my version of fixers. Had Neville said no? Because the prospect of walking under those conditions had its own intrigue and drama. Helluva scene, really. Good plot and action. Armed men versus animals. The certainty of making contact. I could not deny the attractions of a good story, a minidrama. Probably nothing would happen to me. A major Rule of Maz—or of any good journalist—of course was to get the story. How did the two rules balance out?

And of course there is little new under the African sun. I was not the first to ponder the ethics of forcing a confrontation for the entertainment of the folks back home. In the early days of film, wildlife features were hugely popular. An American, Paul Rainey, made several successful films in the early twentieth century.[79] What he and most other filmmakers of the time had never done was capture a lion in full, head-on charge. It was a dangerous duty for a white hunter to accept, not just because the lion would be charging the hunter, but because it would be charging the cameraman as well. Finding the lions, provoking the charge, ensuring the right camera angle and the death only of the lion was a formidable task.

The best hunters of the time—brave and legendary men who had their own codes of the bush—turned down Rainey's requests, thinking them suicidal, even when offered rates far beyond their normal fees. It was some time before Rainey met up with Fritz Schindelar, a man with a mysterious past who was said to be an aristocrat and ex-cavalry officer. Whatever his history, his reputation in Kenya was as a skilled and fearless man, the best polo player in the region, who often rode standing on his saddle. He was also a crack shot, with heavy rifle or shotgun, and a regular guy who got along well with aristocrats and gun bearers alike.

He listened to Rainey's proposal, understood the dangers, and accepted. His assignment was to bait a lion by riding his swift polo pony past the animal, then draw it along toward the cameramen who would film the charge. A platoon of hunters would fire on the lion before it harmed the cameramen.

They found scores of lions and killed more than eleven, but none had been filmed at the proper angle or approach to the cameras. Finally, Schindelar believed he had cornered a particularly game lion in a thicket of tall grass and brush. The cameramen set up their gear. The plan was for Schindelar to ride into the brush, goad the lion, and then turn and run the fast, agile polo pony back toward the cameras.

Schindelar charged up to the edge of the grass and then sped away, attempting to lure the lion, to goad it. The lion stayed at bay.

Then Fritz came to the brush at a different angle, not knowing exactly where the lion was, but again hoping to bring it toward the cameras.

Impossibly swift, the lion came from nowhere. Its charge nearly knocked the horse over, and did throw Fritz from the saddle. He recovered his stance and, as the lion charged him, fired both barrels of his gun at point-blank range, missing with both slugs. The lion knocked him to the ground and savaged his abdomen, then turned on the rest of the men. A volley of rifle fire brought the lion to the ground, dead. It took Fritz Schindelar two days to die, despite frantic efforts by Rainey to transport him to a hospital. "My god what a mighty blow" were among his last words.

Was that what I was asking Neville to do? Play Schindelar to my Rainey? I had no camera or filming in mind, but in all other matters the ethical setup was similar. The very real reason for Steve and Neville's concern was not that we would somehow stumble upon a pride of lounging lions, but that they would almost certainly stumble upon us.

At night, the prides don't lounge. They lunge. They move forcefully through the bush in hunting parties that are all business. They may specialize in and prefer one species of prey, but in their nighttime sorties they are opportunistic. They are looking for warthogs, impalas, wildebeests, buffalo, and zebras, or anything else that might turn up—like us.

And almost certainly, they would come upon us. The Kruger lion population is dense. There are more than a hundred prides in Kruger, with seven to thirty lions in each pride and more than two thousand lions total. They weigh anywhere from two hundred fifty to five hundred pounds and can be more than ten feet in length including the tail. They are equipped to charge prey over short distances, and then seize and hold with massive shoulders and muscular front quarters.

They have the equivalent bulk of a linebacker, and they need the proportionately equivalent fuel. Each lion must eat about fifty-six hundred pounds of food a year, or more than one hundred pounds of meat a week. (A human provides, on average, about fifty pounds of meat.)[80]

Lions are ever so well equipped to obtain that sort of poundage by killing very large animals. Long fangs and sharp claws can quickly kill prey, though neither weapon is always the direct cause of death. The swat of a paw often does the trick to smaller animals. (Imagine taking a sucker punch in the temple from a four-hundred-pound heavyweight with six-inch, razor-sharp, raking brass knuckles protruding from his fist.) A bite to the neck or the head or chest or spine does the job, of course. But big grazing animals often have their necks broken by a shift of the lion's weight. Smaller antelope often are held by the throat and strangled. Other times, lions might grab larger antelope by the nose and mouth and suffocate them.[81]

Yet the lion's most deadly weapon might not be fangs or claws or muscular bulk but social organization. Lions are the only social cat. As John Khoza remarked when he faced down lions in front of him, "Always there will be lions behind you." Somewhere, back in the antediluvian past, both man and lion learned that social organization benefits the individual. It is not uncommon for solitary cats to attack animals twice their bulk. But working together, a pride can take down large animals—a ton of buffalo, for example—with less risk. Many cats working together to down one large animal that provides many meals has an advantage over many cats on individual hunts downing many smaller animals or risking a solitary attack on a large animal. True, Schaller in his studies at one point questioned that common assessment of the value of social organization, suggesting instead that the sharing of cub care resulted in a higher survival rate. Group hunts, he said, often were less successful than lone hunts.[82]

In either case, the end result was the same: socialization gives the lion an advantage in its predatory niche. On my first safari, I found myself in a Land Rover with an African game ranger and a visiting ranger from India who guided for tigers in his home country. Both men were educated field biologists.

"You've got to answer the question I had when I was ten years old," I tell the two men. "Which is the most ferocious and dangerous cat, the lion or the tiger? Put them together, who wins the fight?"

"There is no doubt that in one-on-one combat," says the African game ranger, "the lion would lose. The Bengal tiger on average weighs about five hundred fifty pounds—a one-hundred-pound weight advantage."

"But," the Indian guide says, "in the real world, if they were somehow in the same range, there is no doubt that the lion would gain the predatory niche. The tiger is mostly a solitary animal, and the lion hunts in prides. There is no doubt that lions would drive tigers from the niche at the top of the food chain."[83]

There are many myths about lions and their relationship with mankind. They run the gamut from cuddly Disneyfications and *Born Free* characters with names to the demonization of man-eaters as deranged psychopaths and evil spirits.

Perhaps the biggest myth is that lions naturally fear men and turn to eating humans only when forced to by injury or old age. Any deviation from this concept is seen by some as aberrant, even criminal, the actions of a psychopathic killer who has broken all rules and is "unnatural" or a "rogue."

The truth is quite different. Certainly, some old, lame lions do eat humans. And injured tigers and leopards may be more prone to eating humans because they have no pride or social structure to fall back on. Most recent leopard attacks on humans in Kruger were attributed to the age of the cat or to the fact that the attacking cat was injured and starving.

But researchers from Chicago's Field Museum—Julian C. Kerbis Peterhans and Thomas Patrick Gnoske—recently concluded that lions eat humans for one main reason.

They can. Hey, they always have.

It is a flip oversimplification of their conclusion, but not by much. The main diet of ancient lions in fact was hominids and ungulates— early humans, apes, and antelope. Our forebears were not an accidental appetizer or side dish. They were a main course.

"For most of their history, extinct and living humans have represented little more than a vulnerable, slow-moving, bipedal source of protein for big cats," said Peterhans, who is associate professor of Natural Science at Roosevelt University in Chicago, a Field Museum adjunct curator, and coauthor of the study on man-eating lions published in the *Journal of East African Natural History*.

Over time, social organization and technology changed that. But it took a good long time. Mankind did not one day discover fire and the club, flick a Bic, and drive all of liondom to the desert.

In a paper on cats, evolution, and sociability, Randall Eaton suggested a few years back that early man was at best "co-dominant" with lions for many centuries. So daunting a competitor was the lion that early men fought among themselves, favoring "intraspecific" warfare. In other words, tribes of men fought each other for turf because that was easier than taking on another species as tough as the lion.

"We had millions of years during which we were vulnerable lip-smacking delicacies," write Hart and Sussman. "We've had only a flick of the eye during which we have entered some domination over the predators."

Stone, sticks, fire, then bronze, then iron, steel, gunpowder, bullets, traps, snares, poison, dogs, horses, language, and human social organization eventually prevailed. Most modern-day lions have learned to avoid man—the spear-bearing Masai, the rifle-toting hunter. Yet all this is learned behavior. Even twenty-five thousand years ago, writes G. L. Smuts, the Kruger naturalist, Cro-Magnon man was having a tough time with lions and was far from dominant. In evolutionary terms, this is the blink of an eye. Lions very quickly learn to hunt man when the sense of danger disappears and opportunity presents itself.

"The question most people ask is I would say turned about?" Edwards says. "It is not really a question of why lions would eat people? Look at man, look at me. What do I have? Dull teeth? Short fingernails? No hide, no hair to speak of. I cannot run fast. I cannot smell the air well. I have no hard hooves or anything really that could do harm to an animal.

"So the question really isn't why lions would eat people," he says. "The question is why would they *not* eat people."

Peterhans and Gnoske concluded much the same thing when they said, dryly, "To call such behavior 'aberrant' may be acceptable from an anthropogenic perspective but is 'normal' behavior for the relevant predator."[84]

"Let's take stock of what we can about early humans," wrote anthropologists Hart and Sussman. "They were tasty items for cats, dogs, bears, hyenas, raptors and reptiles."[85]

The proof of this in modern times is brutally clear but not widely known. In Tanganyika, in the 1930s and 1940s, three generations of a lion pride hunted men, women, and children so systematically that they treated villages like pantries. When hungry, the pride would enter a village, select a hut, tear through the roof, and eat the inhabitants as casually as we might open and eat a tin of nuts. George Rushby, the famous white hunter who eventually killed most of the lions, found the animals to be in their prime, with luxuriant, silky coats. The lions had so "selected" humans as the preferred species that a lion would charge through a herd of cattle—and kill only the herdsman.[86]

The famous man-eaters of Tsavo, a pair of male lions that might have killed as many as one hundred thirty-five railroad workers, similarly were found by researchers to have been capable hunters of "normal prey." For a number of reasons, the pair had learned to hunt and eat humans and did so just as if mankind were a tribe of slow and dull-witted warthogs. In each of these cases, it seems as if the lions involved truly were man-eaters, that they had selected humans as a favored prey species, not just taken a human as the opportunity arose.

The selection of a favored prey then is passed along through a generation or more of lions. Authors Chris Harvey and Pieter Kat found that similar prides might develop vastly different preferences based on coincidence. In the Mogogelo region of Botswana, a pride had learned to hunt and prefer baboons—highly unusual behavior in lions. The writers' theory is that the pride discovered that baboons would flee to a tree upon seeing a lion but would jump to the ground if one charging lion started to climb the tree. This lesson led to easy meals for the pride, and they used the trick to make baboons one of their main sources of meat.

Yet in nearby Santawani, a lion pride virtually ignores baboons and seeks more traditional prey. Once, a baboon missed a branch, fell from a height, and died directly in front of the Santawani pride. The lions sniffed the carcass but simply did not connect baboons with meat. They moved on, leaving the body untouched.[87]

In each of the famous man-eater cases, humans helped the situation immeasurably by ignoring the Law of Unintentional Consequences. In Tanganyika, men seeking to control the spread of livestock disease shot all the natural game to form a miles-wide, disease-free buffer. The lions ate what they could: first cattle, then us. Tribespeople were psychologically disarmed from defending themselves because they believed in a lion version of werewolves. The African version of lycanthropy was this: the man-eaters were not mortal. They were men changed into lion demons by shamans who wanted to punish the tribespeople.

In Tsavo, it helped that human endeavor had for decades, perhaps centuries, "provisioned" the lions with humans as food. The slave caravan routes passed through, with a horrible toll. Those who were sick were abandoned. Lions learned to scavenge the corpses. It was an easy step for the cats to take a weak or dying human—and next, perfectly healthy specimens. The caravans kept coming, decade after decade, marking a trail through the jungle of the dead and dying. It was almost as if the caravans were chumming for man-eaters, then training them to eat humans. As if that were not enough incentive, white hunters soon shot out all the elephants for ivory. Without elephants to graze the land, a thick carpet of nearly impenetrable thorn bushes sprang up. The lions moved through this perfect cover at ease; the humans could not.

But the slave caravans did not pass through Kruger and there are more than enough elephants. Neither has the game been eliminated. Far from it. Natural "provisions" should supply adequate meat. An abundance of natural game occurs.

And yet, lions kill humans in Kruger with regularity. The land we are driving on now is a nocturnal killing ground, of that there is no doubt. Lions, like other predators, instinctively take the easy prey. And the easiest prey these days quite often is a refugee.

All of that makes a compelling argument for staying out of the park at night, save for two classes of people: desperate refugees and over-earnest journalists. For a journalist, the worse it sounded, the more attractive was the prospect. Despite the conversation with Neville, despite Steve's flat-out rejection of the proposal, I noodle the idea of walking through the park at night. If not Neville or Steve, perhaps the next guy we were visiting would be my man. Perhaps he was the better "fixer." After all, he was, by all accounts, the Wolhuter of his age.

Chapter 7

THE NEW WOLHUTER

We meet a modern-day Wolhuter; his dangerous brush
with a young lion; the problems of explaining lions; his
unpopularity with modern greens.

Steve, Neville, Suzanne, and I leave John Khoza behind; he, his
daughter Coley, and Paddy and Pauline Buckmaster all stand on the
front steps of the lodge, appearing as a happy family saying good-bye
to dear relatives. They wave, and we wave back until we can no longer
see them. Two giraffes are munching tree canopy leaves in the yard
and form a sort of makeshift arch and gate as we drive away.

"We never did hear all the cobra stories," I say to Neville. He
stays quiet.

Then he grimaces slightly and tells one. When they were young,
Steve and Neville would take a black light out into the bush. The
black light reflected off rocks containing minerals that Steve's father
was mining, and the boys would hurry to retrieve the rocks. The
problem was that the area had nearly as many cobras as rocks.

To teach the boys a lesson, Steve's father found some rocks near a
very large cobra and then irritated the cobra with a stick. It rose, hood
spread, swaying back and forth, to and fro, in the black light, leaving
an indelible impression on the young boys. It was enough to teach
even Steve and Neville to be wary when searching for minerals and to

let them know how close their nighttime expeditions may have lead them to death.

Shortly before we left, Pauline told us perhaps the most recent story. Neville had stepped outside the very room we were staying in and saw a spitting cobra. The weather was cool, the snake sluggish, and Neville by this time was so accustomed to them that in one motion he stooped, grabbed its tail, and flipped it safely into the bush, without breaking stride as he walked toward morning coffee.

It is the third story, we are told, that is the hair-raiser and why Neville grimaces each time we ask him for cobra stories.

We ask again. We get a grimace. Neville says, "Later?" as he cranks the wheel. I press him good-naturedly, but Neville demurs. "This one? It is not going to make me look very smart?" he says.

Gibson smiles wolfishly. Always the silent type, a man of few words unless asked a question, Steve can at times be heard chuckling ever so slightly to himself.

"Refugee stories" has a check next to it on my safari itinerary, "Last cobra story" a question mark. What pops up next on the list sounds simple, but isn't: "Possible solutions, new Beowulf."

There is a man, Steve Gibson and Neville Edwards tell me, whose modern tale is not unlike Wolhuter's.

Today, there are still people like Wolhuter and Stevenson-Hamilton fighting the "lion wars"—both metaphorically in the sense of politics and "information," and literally in the sense of physical struggle. Neville and Steve drive us outside the park into Mpumalanga Province to meet a man who has fought in both manners and might be, if anyone is, the modern equivalent of Wolhuter. I am open to the possibility that this is my new great hunter, the man who can slay the system.

He looks the part. Gerrie Camacho stands six foot four and if you look closely and already know his story, you can see the scars on his leg and arms. They are not disfiguring; in fact, in this part of the country, they are something of a badge of honor. Gerrie is the chief scientist of the Mpumalanga Parks Board, the coveted equivalent of being head field researcher for all state parks in, say, Montana or Idaho or Alaska. His curriculum vitae says officially, "Zoologist (Scientific Specialized Terrestrial Fauna Projects)," but everyone knows he is a lion man.

I meet him when our safari vehicle bumps into the dusty courtyard of the Mpumalanga Parks Conservation District a few miles west of Kruger National Park. Cages of a size to house large cats line the courtyard. A Land Rover truck is parked in front of a house that serves as district offices. Flowers have been planted by families who live here, and a child's tricycle spans a sidewalk. Screen doors are on old-fashioned springs that allow a door to yawn open slowly, then bang shut brusquely as the spring reclaims its shape. The compound has the feel of a midwestern farm, with outbuildings, garages, labs, and storage structures huddled close together amid the vastness of farmland, ranch land, and veld on either side.

There is little to suggest that this is ground zero of the new lion war zone, and in fact for the most part the wars Camacho fights are quite different from the ones Wolhuter and Stevenson-Hamilton waged against poachers.

Yet the quiet scene may be the best place to get some of my most pressing questions answered.

More specifically: who has a shot at changing the new state of affairs and forging a new covenant among refugees and lions? And of getting me into the park at night?

Camacho is softspoken and understated about his role in current lion controversies. He seems one part rugged bushman and one part bemused professor and both traits serve him well. For the most part, the wars fought these days are soft wars, "information wars" against ignorance and prejudice. What is different about the new information wars is that they now skew toward informing the public of their *positive* prejudices toward lions and not just the historic negative perceptions. A hundred years ago, lions were seen as God-cursed. Today, they are seen as blessed by God and ready to lie down with the lambs.

Once Camacho spent most of his time convincing skeptical ranchers that repopulating areas of South Africa with lions was a good thing. He still does, and notes that while the Kruger lion population seems fine, the worldwide population is decreasing drastically. He is most certainly a pro-lion sort of guy.

But now he has found himself in the odd position of warning middle-class tourists and residents of nearby communities of the dangers of lions. The tendency of a green-leaning public is to treat lions as friends and forget they are wild carnivores.

Of particular concern to Gerrie is the community of Marloth Park, the suburbanlike development just south of Kruger and home to Izinyoni Lodge. Some of the other residents, not Paddy Buckmaster, show a dangerous tendency to treat lions casually—as if they were squirrels or raccoons or finches at a bird feeder. His fear is that the Marloth residents are unintentionally creating a new breed of man-eating lions. The affluent white homeowners who cherish the lions in their backyards during the daytime are well meaning, and their dedication to nature seems sincere.

But the lions move among the houses at night and sometimes pick off the help and perhaps the occasional thief. Camacho has even suggested removing the lions, but the residents will not hear of it. He wonders if some of the lions already have learned such bad habits that they should be put down.

It is ironic for Camacho to favor the restriction or killing of lions. He has raised lion cubs in his home and become very attached to individual animals. He can see the distinct personalities of the lions he observes. For more than ten years Camacho has worked at reintroducing lions to the wild outside Kruger and might spend an entire year trying to build a self-sustaining pride for release, knowing the lions not just by their markings but by their movements and moods. He truly loves the species.

People on both sides tend to listen to him, not only because he is a scientist with communication skills, but because he has real scars from the lion war.

Bands of shiny tissue run along his arms and right leg, and in the course of a conversation about lions Camacho sometimes will lightly knead his healed wounds with one hand as he makes a point with the other. The locals respect those scars. Anyone treated that way by a lion who still is their advocate demands respect.

The situation for Camacho years back was this: for days in the winter of 1988, in a private area just outside Kruger, Camacho and others had been attempting to dart and treat a pregnant lioness who seemed infected. They had lured her into a large fenced-in area, but always the pride followed her. One day in July, helpers called excitedly to tell him the pride had left the area, but the sick lioness and one young male remained.

Camacho and Johan Vander Walt, a conservation worker, piled into the Land Rover and rushed to the area. Vander Walt parked at the fence entrance to prevent the pride from reentering. Camacho hurried to the lioness on foot, thinking to scare away the one young male. Young males are skittish and, sure enough, Camacho, at six foot four, had only to approach it and yell, flapping his arms. The young male rushed away toward the pride and the hole in the fence and all was well.

Something turned him, though. Perhaps it was the Land Rover. Perhaps he lost sight of the fence gap. Escape blocked, or so it must have seemed, he wheeled and charged back toward Camacho.

There, Gerrie Camacho made his stand. The stand is all important to check mock charges, and now he hooted and waved as the young male neared. He "looked large," as large as he could, with his hands above his head.

But this was no mock charge. The male hit Camacho and knocked the big man backward, as if he were an aluminum can struck by a flying anvil.

It was at that moment that Camacho learned a fact known by only a select few people: the one good point about being eaten by a lion is that sometimes it does not seem to hurt much.

Dr. David Livingstone, the explorer and missionary, was seized in 1844 by a lion and wrote later, "He caught my shoulder as he sprang and we both came to the ground below together. Growling horribly close to my ear, he shook me as a terrier dog does a rat. The shock produced a stupor similar to that which seems to be felt by a mouse after the first shake of the cat. It caused a sort of dreaminess, in which there was no sense of pain, nor feeling of terror, though I was quite conscious of all that was happening. . . . The shake annihilated fear and allowed no sense of horror in looking round at the beast. The peculiar state is probably produced in all animals killed by the carnivora; and if so, is a merciful provision by our benevolent Creator for lessening the pain of death."[88]

Harry Wolhuter did not experience this, of course, but hunter-writer Peter Capstick described an identical rush and daze when he was knocked to the ground by a lion. His African sidekick distracted the lion, which then knocked the poor man to the ground and chomped down on his arm. Capstick rose from his reverie, retrieved a weapon, and killed the lion, saving the man who had saved him, but not before noting the look on the face of his trusted colleague. As the lion savaged him, Capstick's colleague wore a blissful smile, very much at peace.[89]

Cynthia Dusel-Bacon, a geologist, described her mauling by a black bear in less beatific terms, but her experience sixty miles south of Fairbanks, Alaska, seems close to the others. She played dead when the bear approached, which is a good move if the bear is simply defensive and not predatory.

But this bear was predatory and began eating her right arm. Not just biting it. Eating it. "I was completely conscious of feeling my flesh torn, teeth against bone, but the sensation was more of a numb horror at what was happening to me than of a specific reaction to each bite," she said.

In fact, she had the calm presence of mind to take a radio out of her backpack and, as the bear continued chewing on her arm, say to her base camp almost routinely, "Ed, this is Cynthia. Come quick, I'm being eaten by a bear." She lost both arms to the bear and it was chewing on her skull before the chopper arrived. Still she experienced little immediate pain.[90]

"They're absolutely right!" Camacho said of these accounts, as if the men and woman were students who had made a profound and unexpected observation.

"You do *feel* everything. It is as if you have been seized by a vise. Such strength! You know you are powerless against it. You feel your muscle ripping and tearing. You feel your meat separate from the bone. You *feel* all that, but you do not feel pain or really care. You are in a dream state, not unpleasant at all."

The other fortunate matter was that the lion had knocked Camacho against a tree. He did not go down. If he had, he would have been killed. The lion seized and worried Camacho's right calf in the vise of his teeth and mauled his upper body with box-cutterlike claws. Periodically, the lion would attempt to move its grip upward, up toward Camacho's softer parts, for the kill.

Camacho, meanwhile, fought the daze and began pummeling the lion's eyes. "It was the only soft spot I could reach, you see." He hit the animal with big roundhouse lefts and rights. And whenever the lion tried to move its grip up, Camacho would pull with his leg. The smell of the lion—a sweet and powerful odor of urine and defecation—was all about him, engulfing him.

Vander Walt watched in horror, but was more horrified when the pride, triggered by the sounds of the attack, began streaming toward the hole in the fence, on a sortie line to Camacho. This would make short work of Camacho, Vander Walt knew, and he looked in the

Land Rover. Normally, they would have a rifle, at least a .375 H&H, clipped to the dash. In backup, Camacho sometimes carried a .357 magnum revolver with an eight-inch barrel holstered on his belt.

But they had been hurried. They had had one shot at isolating the lioness. They had rushed. The pistol was back on the table. So now, as he desperately searched the Landie, Vander Walt came up with . . . a tire iron.

The lion pride rushed toward the hole in the fence to join the young male lion attacking Camacho. Vander Walt grabbed the metal tool, jumped from the Land Rover, and ran toward the hole, waving the tire iron. He made as much noise as he could and looked as "large" as he could. Still, it is not recommended practice to charge a pride of charging lions.

This time, it worked. The pride wheeled and retreated, confused and stymied. Then Vander Walt charged back toward Camacho and the young lion yelling and again swinging the tire iron. Camacho was still pummeling the lion, swinging great, powerful roundhouses as the lion clawed his thighs and lower arms, tried to get Camacho in a clinch, and move its bite upward to softer, vulnerable zones.

In the end, it was all too much for the young male. The punches. The madman with the tire iron. The pride retreating. He let loose of Camacho, who immediately wrenched his leg free. The male lit out for the hole in the fence, and it was over.

Camacho, still pumped and in a dream, thanked Vander Walt for his kindness, limped to the Land Rover, and asked to be driven back to the office, as he still had lots of work to do. Vander Walt looked at Camacho's leg and saw a calf muscle that drooped downward. On Camacho's thigh, four severed tendons stuck up like stiff, busted banjo strings. On one arm, exposed tendons had looped up, like bunched shoestrings doubled in their eyelets.

"Ah, yes, very good and of course, Gerrie, the office," Vander Walt told him. "But perhaps we should stop by the hospital *just* for a moment to prevent infection."

A half hour later Camacho was in severe pain. Sixty-four stitches later, and after weeks of rehab and healing, he was back in the field searching for lions—but not vengeance.

"In no way could that lion be held at fault," Camacho says. "I was stupid. I caused the attack.

"I was stupid," he says again. "Always, when you are around lions, you are working a thin edge. But you become too comfortable, you assume."

The drama of the mauling played somewhat like Wolhuter's encounter—on a minor scale. It received no worldwide publicity, largely because Camacho is a modest and private man. But the story is known by those who count. When Camacho speaks, people listen. He never talks about his injuries unless asked, but everyone knows. Ranchers, rangers, tourists, and conservationists hear him out. It does not hurt, either, that Camacho physically spans the world of the wild and of science. At his six-four height, all but the largest Boer rancher must look up to him.

But despite the credits he has built up, he has had little sway with the greener residents of the greater Kruger area. If ranchers once demonized lions, greens now tend to beatify them. A whole generation has grown up with Walt Disney versions of lions and views them as friendly, cuddly animals. The teen daughter of a friend, watching a lion take down a zebra, asked once, "Is the lion hugging the zebra, Daddy?" Early visitors to Kruger often protested lion kills and sometimes forced rangers to scare the cruel lions away from the innocent antelope. Some tourists always will want to leave the Land Rover. For those who have watched too many reruns of *Born Free*, Camacho suggests they might be in danger of making their own movie titled *Die Young*. The greens, in short, often have as much poor information now about lions as the bubba-rancher set did a century ago. They are both wrong about lion behavior, at one-hundred-eighty-degree opposites of the political compass.

While Camacho spends much of his time warning the Marloth Park people of the dangers of lions, he remains concerned about the growing reputation of the Kruger lions as man-eaters.

"Yes, what you are saying about the lions and refugees is true, but please, in my opinion, you must not be sensational and call them man-eaters," he says, shortly into an "information wars" session with me. "Or to say that they 'have a taste for human flesh.' They are not man-eaters in the sense of legend. They do not specialize in man. There are things that occur naturally, where lions will attack man and perhaps eat him. But that is different than being a man-eater, a lion that actively seeks out humans."

Always, Camacho tells the Marloth Park crowd, you must understand that "you are on a thin edge" when around lions. He repeats that phrase—thin edge—wherever he goes. Always, it must be kept in mind, he says, that the lion is two animals. Man is diurnal and sees the lion in its daytime passive mode. The night belongs to the lion, though, and there the lion is a fearsome predator. It is not evil. It is an opportunistic carnivore that walks the bush in highly organized hunting parties looking for protein. At night, it is a biological bot, a near-perfect killing machine. Quickly, if there is a new form of easy prey, it will learn to kill it.

And always, it must be remembered, there are two conditions in which humans can become lion prey. The first is when they intrude on the "comfort zone" of the lion. Even the passive daytime tabbies will attack if someone in Kruger is foolish enough to leave the car and stick a motor drive in their face. Like Hannibal Lechter, they tend to eat the rude.

The second condition is when something in human behavior triggers the lion to attack. The attack trigger seems hardwired into the lion psyche, and, like kittens to a dangled string, they respond aggressively to some signals.

"I have been in a Land Rover in daytime just a meter away from a very placid lioness when a small child cried," Camacho says. "*Instantly* she was alert, searching for the sign of weakness she had heard. She had sensed vulnerability, and you *know* when they look at you when they want you for food.

"They are experts in spotting weakness, in seeing differences," he continues. "This is how they pick their prey from a herd. Constantly, they are scanning for vulnerability."

Camacho is the lion's best friend, but even he is worried about the deadly toll of refugees. In part, he fears a backlash. But he does not fall among those conservationists who make excuses for the lions or suggest alternative explanations. He does not do this for several reasons, and one reason is that, like Neville, he has come face to face, literally, with the "refugee problem." He learned all too well that it is much easier to think of that problem in the abstract than to confront a body in the night in Kruger Park.

Camacho was in the field in July 1998, outdoors in the bush of Kruger with two American veterinarian trainees and a camera crew run by Greg Nelson documenting Camacho's work for a video series called *Free of Fear*. They had baited and called in lions with loud-speakers blaring the loopy sounds of hyena, but had darted only two members of the pride. This method always worked for the whole pride. So where was the rest of the pride?

Someone on the camera crew swore he heard a human cry from the road, not three hundred yards away, but when they listened again, they heard nothing, and the scientists discounted it. Camacho grew restless. What was keeping the rest of the pride? They had two lions down, doped out, but soon they would be arising. So out went the scientists to find the pride.

They did not have to go far. Just three hundred yards away, off to the side of the road, was the fed-upon corpse of a refugee. It was clear from the tracks what had happened. First the spoor, the tracks, of the refugee, wearing an athletic-type shoe with the brand name raised on the sole. Slow, casual steps in the dust of the road, imprinting the brand name at each step. Goin' west to Jonni, surely but slowly. Then, a bit farther, following behind, the tracks of a large lioness emerge from the bush, as if merging from an entrance ramp, and begin following. The two sets of footprints proceed for a while unchanged, the shoe imprints spaced at a leisurely pace, the lion pug marks following, no more hurriedly, claws retracted, in lion cruising mode. She seems curious at this point, judging from her gait, open to opportunity, but her claws are still sheathed.

Then, the shoe tracks veer to the side. There is a scattering of stone and dust as the shoes twist and then break into a run. He must have heard her; perhaps she growled or coughed. And the lion tracks show the trigger point: instantly, the slow walk becomes a short, bounding run, then a leap. There is an area of scuffle. Both the man's shoes are stripped loose and thrown to the side. But he is up. The refugee regains his feet and, barefoot, races for his life and a tree that is not there. The lion tracks—these with claws extended now—follow for the shortest of distances. And then there is a great deal of blood. The camera catches up with the corpse, and it is a smear of red and rib bone, teeth exposed through missing lips in a rictus smile.

The Western men of science are repulsed and shocked. They must pull the Land Rover over the corpse to keep animals away from it. And amid the sense of sadness now comes too a sense of fear. Men who have spent dozens of nights, hundreds some of them, sleeping in the open bush now are sincerely afraid of lions for the first time.

Camacho, the veteran, is so shaken by the corpse he literally staggers away. One glimpse and, like Neville Edwards, he feels an overwhelming need just to get away from the corpse, to avoid contact, to avoid having to bag it or analyze it or have anything to do with it. Dazed, he walks through the bush, three hundred yards back toward the darting. He stumbles first upon one darted lion, literally stepping on her, changes directions, and then bumps into the other, which is recovering now, eyeing him warily. Camacho regains his senses and walks back to the group assembled around the corpse. There is too much gear to return home. They must sleep in the bush. They circle the Land Rovers, pioneer style, and Camacho chooses to sleep *under* his. It is a fitful sleep for this man of science, filled with nightmares about lion attacks and smiling corpses.

"Yet, again, this was not the 'fault' of the lion," Camacho says. "The lion did not seek the refugee. The refugee walked into her turf and triggered behavior in the lion. You cannot call her a 'man-eater' in the classic sense of the word."

The answer is not in killing the lions, he says. The answer is somehow to change the route of the migration or to educate the immigrants— and the help at Marloth Park—about how to avoid the lions.

But how one does that is beyond one's control, and it is officially beyond the control of anyone in the park. The immigration policy is rock hard and unchangeable: the immigrants must be stopped. They are "work thieves" who take South African jobs from South Africans. They have no legal standing in the park. They enter at their own risk and suffer the consequence. That is the de facto policy of the government. And the Marloth Park residents? Some few think the lions make dandy watchdogs and help keep the area crime-free at night. Others think the attacks on humans are anomalies.

Camacho sees both the immigrants' plight and the philosophy of Marloth as one day endangering the animals he loves. The lions are not true man-eaters yet, he says, but the trend of both the refugee policy and the Marloth pro-lion zoning could turn large populations of lions into true man-eaters.

"The lions are attacking the servants walking at night now," he says. "But if this continues, it is inevitable that one of the residents or their children will be attacked."

"Oh, they are fine with the lions in Marloth right now," Paddy Buckmaster had said when we were at Izinyoni Lodge. "But let's see how they feel when the first white grandchild is picked off the front porch."

The backlash from something like that could be brutal to the lions. Camacho knows this and fears it, but aside from dispersing information, there is little he can do. The greens of Marloth not only do not take his counsel, when he attempts to move the lions back to their Kruger home, they fight him tooth and nail. A part of me understands that. A part of me would like to live in Marloth Park and see the lions walking through my backyard. But a part of me understands why that's not such a hot idea.

I don't even think about asking Camacho about guiding me through the park. The last thing he needs—assuming a lion would eat one at all—is a partly consumed journalist to deal with. Camacho does great work and labors mightily. But he is not the man to slay this monster. He is as good and respected as they come, but for change to occur, it would take an aroused or at least a sympathetic citizenship.

It's been true of every investigative story or project I've undertaken where change occurs. Reform happens only when the citizenry truly understands the problem in an emotional, accurate, factual but heartfelt manner.

That was true years back in my nation's dispute over slavery as well. A famous work of fiction, *Uncle Tom's Cabin*, fueled the passion of abolitionists to fight our apartheid in the United States.

And my thought was that surely there have been enough true stories in South Africa to melt the heart of any antirefugee sentiment. I just need to find them.

Chapter 8

UNCLE TOM'S LIONS

We examine the mysterious northern part of the park, where most of the killings have occurred; power lines serve as a guide for the refugees but also for the lions; the desperate trip of Johanna Nkuna and her three children; her brave act of sacrifice; her daughter's survival in a termite mound; the response of the park and the rangers.

We are still waiting for the grand finale of Neville Edwards's cobra stories as we speed along paved roads within Kruger. And he is still saving the finale for another day. Instead, we talk about the north of the park and the main Kruger camp there, Punda Maria.

"We do not know that place well?" Neville says as we roll through Kruger. "I do not know if we want to know that place well."

Indeed, the northern part of the park has some of the lightest tourist traffic and some of the heaviest refugee traffic. And it was here that the refugees first gained any sort of sympathetic profile with the public. It was here that a heartbreaking case, a case that cut across class, race, and nationality, so shocked the country that, like the fictional *Uncle Tom's Cabin*, it might have aroused the populace to do the right thing by the refugees.

The north park to this day is a place of superstition and Western misunderstanding. The addition of the northern part of the park helped turn what was then the Sabi Sands Reserve into the modern footprint of Kruger. It is said that the Lebombo Hills, at the eastern edge of the park, hard against Mozambique, are haunted by two ghosts, white men on white horses. One is supposed to be an officer killed in the Boer War. The other is said to be a nineteenth-century Englishman who shot seven elephants in one day, left the tusks in place to loosen overnight, and never returned. He is thought to have been the victim of poachers. He rides the hills at night, it is said, seeking his ivory and vengeance upon his murderers.[91]

Punda Maria itself was named for what the first ranger there, Captain J. J. Coester, thought was Swahili for "zebra." He was wrong. The Swahili name is punda milia—"striped donkey." Coester's apologists argue that the Brit knew this full well but had a wife, Maria, who was fond of striped dresses and actually intended the name as a wry joke, naming the camp "striped Maria."

The problem with that is that while punda milia means striped donkey, Punda Maria does not mean striped Maria. It means Maria the donkey. It is not the first African nuance that smug Westerners have misunderstood.[92]

In the north, too, are the myths of the enormous baobab trees. In winter, leafless, they seem to be turned upside down, their roots waving in the air. This is said by some to occur because devils inhabit baobab and God turned the tree upside down to punish the spirits for lording it over other trees.

Some African people sing when they pass the baobab so as not to hear the voices of spirits. Others say you can hear the spirits laughing if you put your ear to the trunk of a baobab. Still others, ominously, one supposes in the context of our story, say the flowers contain spirits, and anyone who picks them will be eaten by a lion.[93]

By 1998, if the legend is true, then many people were picking many flowers from the baobab, because many people were being eaten in the north.

By this time, there was no war in Mozambique, but the country was still war-ravaged. A truce in 1992 had sent a great rush of refugees fleeing across the park as Renamo loosened its hold on villagers. Meanwhile, the international community concentrated on repatriation of the displaced Mozambicans, even though Mozambique itself had not been restored to provide the basics of life. The economy had not recovered from two decades of fighting; droughts in the early '90s helped kill whatever crops and cattle remained. In Magude, before the war, 200,000 cattle graced the district. Only 2,000 survived the conflict. So repatriated Mozambicans, or those displaced internally from their villages, found nothing for them when they came home.[94]

In South Africa, by contrast, apartheid was dead, and evermore it was said that South Africa was the America of Africa—a land of opportunity and freedom.

So it was, in those conditions, that eleven-year-old Emelda Nkuna and her family set out one day in July 1998 from the small village of Shikwalakwala. Her mother, Johanna, and Emelda's two older sisters were bound through Kruger to Soweto, where an uncle lived. There, in the famous township of South Africa, considered a center of poverty by many, lay hope.[95]

Crossing into the Kruger was no problem. Once, the fence carried a lethal thirty-thousand-volt charge said to have claimed the lives of nearly one hundred.[96] But the charge had been turned off four years before by postapartheid South Africa. Animals and poachers regularly forged passageways through the fence. The girls and their mother slipped through without trouble and walked toward the setting sun, goin' west to Jonni.

In the south of the park, refugees move on the little-traveled road near the Crocodile River. In the middle section, they cut right through the bush near Satara. But to the north, near Punda Maria, where the Nkuna family traversed, the habit was to follow the Caborra Bassa power lines, which snake across the remote bush country.

The lines are an aid to navigation for the refugees, but also, some say, a chow line for lions.[97] It is not hard to see how this happened. For the past thirty years, the refugee columns had been not a few hundred healthy Mozambicans seeking opportunity in South Africa, but thousands—tens of thousands—of weak, sick, starving people stumbling toward any relief they could find. When lions were "vermin," the big cats fled for their lives when they saw any human. As they became more protected, they stopped fleeing at the sight of tourists in daytime. As the migration of refugees switched from diurnal to nocturnal, behavior changed again. The trigger points of lion behavior naturally kicked in to play. It was possible for a small stream of refugees to pass through the park irregularly without much damage being done. There were encounters, similar to John's first trip, but if the refugees took the "stand" as John did, there were fewer deaths. The Shangan then retained bush craft and knew how to deal with lions. Moreover, there probably were not enough encounters for the lions to learn to hunt humans or that the power lines meant a steady supply of prey.

But the civil war of the 1970s, and the 1980s and early 1990s, joined with the other pestilence, changed all that. In those years, the refugee columns were not a few hundred healthy Mozambicans seeking opportunity in South Africa. They were tens of thousands of sick, starving, weak people, some dying on their feet, most just stumbling forward. They fled blindly without caution.

"So at night," Camacho told me during one interview, "if you are a refugee, the lions will size you up. If you are too small, you are vulnerable. If you are overweight, you are vulnerable. If you limp, you are vulnerable. If you are alone, you are vulnerable. If you are any of these things, then you may trigger a lion attack. It is the same to the lions as if you are a squealing pig.

"They do not set out to hunt humans, but if every night there is predictably a large group of vulnerable refugees, the lions will see that there is easy prey. So long as there is easy prey, they will kill it and this will stay in their memory. They do not set out to kill humans. The humans cross their territory and trigger the behavior."

* * *

There is no doubt that lions were nearby the night the Nkuna family came down those power lines. The family had fared well for most of the trip, but in the bush near Punda Maria they heard noises and growls. A pride was hunting. The lions advanced on the small band, snarling at the girls, heading instinctively toward the young and the weak, testing for vulnerability.

It was a very brave thing that Johanna Nkuna did then. It is not recommended by lion experts, who say the stand you make against a lion is all important in such situations. They will say that you should never run. Never threaten the lions either. But few of the lion experts are mothers and none of them were there that night near Punda. It was just Johanna Nkuna, the mother of three girls, and lions who were attempting to steal and eat her grown babies.

The brave thing that Johanna Nkuna did as she faced the lions was as ageless as time itself on the timeless African veld. She charged the lions, yelling and waving her hands.[98]

It worked for Vander Walt and his tire iron in daytime to save Camacho. But it did not work for Johanna Nkuna with a pride on the hunt at night. The lions took her down and made short work of her.

Her sacrifice gave the children a chance. The three sisters scattered, running for their lives. The two older girls fled east, found each other, and ran along the lines back toward home.

Emelda Nkuna raced a short distance and instinctively ducked into a small hole in a very large termite mound. From there, she huddled for the night and heard the awful noises. Her mother's screams. The lions' snarls and growls. And then the more horrible quiet.

The next day, she crept out to find the mostly eaten body of her mother. Lions do what lions do. They consume the viscera of most animals first, which is curious because of the lower protein content. Some scientists believe the lions find needed sources of fat in these organs. They then move to the denser muscles. For reasons not fully known, they often do not eat the pubic areas of humans. Nor are they fond of heads with hair. The remains of Johanna Nkuna were either skeleton or simply gone. What was left sent the girl into severe shock.

Young Emelda Nkuna walked away from that horror aimlessly, along a nearby road. A safari vehicle filled with tourists and a ranger pulled even, matching her slow pace. She neither acknowledged them nor fled nor stopped walking nor replied to questions asked in English. "What are you doing alone in the park?" a ranger asked finally in the Xitsonga language. And slowly the story came out.

The incident made the papers. For a brief period, it seemed as if the story would be the *Uncle Tom's Cabin* for refugees—a tale so heartbreaking and compelling that a popular movement would form. For a short time, Emelda did become the poster child for the refugees' plight. There was talk of killing lions again, of lion justice, and talk too of liberalizing the immigration laws.

But talk soon faded. Perhaps if it had been captured on film, the world would have awakened. But a few weeks passed and Emelda was deported back to her small village in Mozambique, and that was that.

I ask those who work with refugees how I might find her. They say it is of little use to try to reach her in her village. She and her sisters already will have attempted to cross the park again. They will either have succeeded or been captured and deported. Or they will have joined their mother.

I ask Neville and Steve if they could find her. I'd be glad to pay them—and her. "Is it possible?" Neville said. "I doubt it. We could go there? But without you. A lot of AKs still out there. A million mines?"

"Even if we got there," Steve adds, "everyone will claim to be her even if they are not, once the word gets out that there are Westerners with money for stories."

After a spate of news articles in 1997 and 1998, it became rare to see reports of lion killings in the local newspapers. Neville's sighting of the poor woman in 2000, for example, never made the papers. Nor did Camacho's discovery of the man that night. Few incidents are reported, and record keeping by the park is hit and miss.

Besides, the lions and refugees were an old story by then. The killing of poor Johanna Nkuna was an oddity worth noting. But other killings? It is a little like the old definition of "news." A man biting a dog is news, not a dog biting a man. Lions biting humans were just too commonplace to stir editors and reporters. Lions eating humans no longer made the evening news.

The half-life of martyrs in Kruger is short, and memory decays within months. In late 2004, park officials directed me to the Punda-area park police for details about the killing of Johanna Nkuna. I gave them the date, location, and name of the victim. They replied that they had never heard of such a case.[99]

Chapter 9

THE NEW ECONOMICS, THE NEW ALL-AFRICA

The relative earning power of a lion and a Mozambican
are quantified and laid out; the hard feelings among
most South Africans toward the Mozambican refugees;
the attempted solutions of the rangers and their failure;
a model for quantifying the slaughter.

Almost no one I spoke with about the refugees on my earlier, tourist
trip was willing to talk at length about the problem. Steve and Neville
accepted readily. Why?

One reason might be that both men are immigrants themselves.
Their boyhood explorations of the bush took place not in South
Africa but in Rhodesia. Like South Africa, Rhodesia was dominated
for much of the twentieth century by a white minority, and a war of
liberation there lasted many years. Their innocent, mischievous days
ended when Neville and Steve, approaching young manhood, were
conscripted into elite elements of the Rhodesian army. Steve was
drafted into Grey's Scouts, a mounted cavalry unit of skilled trackers
and commandos. Neville was conscripted into another unit.

Neither man talks much about those days. The racial strife was
foreign to them. They were accustomed in their bush lives to dealing
with blacks and whites with little distinction. They would strike deals:

you teach us the bush and Zulu, we will teach you English and other skills. Blacks were playmates and friends, not enemies. Both men as youths learned tribal dances that they still perform.

The one part of their military service they do remember vividly and will talk about is leave. The army command tried to stagger leaves among the three main arms of the army to cut down on fights among rival units, such as are common among U.S. units. Imagine Green Berets, Seals, and a Ranger unit or two in the same bar and you get the picture. When a critical mix of competing units is combined with plentiful alcohol and too few women, the resultant chemistry brings a quick brawl and plenty of MPs.

There was a time in the 1970s, though, when the Rhodesian brass messed up and all three branches descended on the same saloon at the same time. Neville spied Steve, and despite their rival affiliations, they embraced and started catching up.

The reunion did not set the proper tone for the evening. Soon, both Neville and Steve were being heckled. Why, Neville was asked, was he talking with a baboon from Grey's? Why, Steve was asked, was he talking with some guy from a rival unit?

They do not remember the exact words that sparked the fight, but, standing back to back, they threw the first punches. Soon one hundred fifty men were going at it, on the main floor, on the second floor, and on the stairs. Taking and giving punches, Neville and Steve heard above the din the sirens of the police and MPs. They knew what that meant. Leave would be cut short; plus, police dogs often were used and bit indiscriminately.

Without a word, the men fought their way up the stairs. Through a second-floor window they could see the police arriving. "Use the police car? As a trampoline?" Neville suggested.

"Bet you a case of beers I can rip off that blue siren," Steve said.

"You're on," Neville replied.

As the police streamed into the bar, the two friends jumped from the second floor, landing on either side of the blue light, popping it clear of its moorings. They both grabbed the light and rushed off into the night. The case of beer is at issue to this day.

But that is the only incident told as a happy remembrance of their military service. Soon, Rhodesia would be history and Zimbabwe would rise in its place. It was not safe for white former military personnel, even conscripts, to remain in the country. In his unpublished memoirs, Steve writes simply:

> After a particular short call-up mission in 1981, we were advised to leave the country. So early in 1982, I bought a train ticket and left my home and my country, bound for South Africa. I left the newly re-born Zimbabwe with one suitcase and a little cash in my pocket. In those days, we were young and had no real responsibilities. A few friends and a couple of my cousins were in the same predicament but we decided to make good out of a bad situation.
>
> We partied on the train all the way to South Africa. A customs official at the border who was checking our passports commented on the fact that my Rhodesian passport was due to expire on that very same day but he let me through anyway.
>
> It was not easy re-settling in South Africa and I was homesick for years to come.

Some years later both he and Neville would know for certain that the sadness was gone and they had resettled when they encountered a particularly cranky rhinoceros. It happened after they had gotten a good foothold in South Africa and knew that "home" was no longer Zimbabwe or the old Rhodesia.

Hold the thought of Steve, Neville, and the cranky rhinoceros for the moment, because it was not just wildlife that allowed them to feel at home in a new country. There was also the economics of wildlife, which among other things made it possible to live and work as they do. The economics of wildlife—along with its handmaiden, the politics of wildlife—explain two other things as well. They explain why Mozambicans live as they do, and why lions are not only an ecological keystone species but an economic keystone of the entire region.

The Kruger, the Mozambicans, and the lions are interrelated in a number of ways, and one way to understand those relationships is with statistics. In search of those numbers, my investigative safari takes a turn again from the literal roads of Africa to a figurative one, where columns on spreadsheets add up to more than their sums. For the economics of wildlife and immigration are as interesting as any literal tracks. Both tell a tale. It is wildlife economics and wildlife politics that I am tracking now. This is a part of the game I like— what used to be called the paper chase. Parts come together in the paper chase, even if it is all a digital chase these days. Dots appear, connect, form lines that underscore the problem and opportunity the park faces.

In the main library of the park at Skukuza is the skin of the lion Harry killed, framed and preserved. You can see knife holes in the chest and throat. Displayed beside the skin is the sheath knife he used. The knife seems incredibly small. If someone handed it to me to carve a roast, I'd ask what else was in the drawer.

I attack the research in the glow of computer spreadsheets and the silence of the library. My hypothesis is simple: any system, good or bad, rests on some sort of economic and social base, and some sort of public policy supports that base, or at least does not interfere with it.

The first question in this library safari is simple. How many refugees succeed, as John did, and how many fall prey to lions, like Johanna Nkuna?

The total number of dead is officially unknown. Nor is it likely to be known. No central records are kept, no running score. Amid the dozens of research projects and theses under way in the park, there are no known biomass or scat studies that would test lions for traces of human consumption. There is no coverup. It's just that no government unit is in charge or wants to be. And like the crazy aunt in the attic, the topic is not one for polite discussion. It would be convenient to assert that the tourist industry has swept the whole thing under the carpet. Capstick once wrote that this was the case regarding lion kills of humans in Africa. "There are several good reasons why, despite the surprising number of maneating incidents that occur today in Africa, most are hushed up like an epidemic of social disease at a bible school," he wrote. "It's the same reason that Florida Chambers of Commerce don't go out of their way to spread the word of shark attacks along their beaches."[100] But in truth tourists are not known to have been seriously harmed in Kruger, and there is no sinister silence or sophisticated spin when questions are asked, just discomfort and uneasiness. And the data—the total number of humans killed by lions—is simply not available.

Why not? Under the apartheid regime, the answer seems obvious. Whites ran the government with little concern for the fate of black Mozambicans.

But why no counts, why no eased immigration laws, postapartheid? That is a more subtle matter. South Africa is in a difficult era, an era of ever so finely counterweighted mobiles of wants and needs and hates and loves, of stirrings and yearnings, of potentials and promises long delayed. The lions and the refugees are two counterweights in that intricate mobile. Change one or the other radically and the mobile could dip and sway precariously.

President Mandela himself had helped set the weights that kept the political mobiles balanced for Kruger. Without his leadership, the park might well be dead and developed into land for farming. As apartheid began to unwind in 1990, there quite literally was a gathering of angry black Africans on the park boundary. The popular cry was to disband the park and parcel out the land. Families who were huddled together in the tin-roofed townships outside Johannesburg could be given farmland in Kruger. This symbol of Afrikaner elitism named after an Afrikaner icon surely would fall. Bush meat would be plentiful for a while as well.

Mandela checked that impulse. Such radical land reform had hardly ever worked in Africa. Urban dwellers in township slums did not convert to successful farmers overnight. Economies, most recently in Zimbabwe, imploded as black settlers or squatters began subsistence farming on land once used for highly efficient agribusiness.[101]

Moreover, Mandela recognized the magnificence of Kruger and knew it was not only important to the heritage of both whites and blacks, but was a worldwide draw for foreign tourists and their hard currencies. "You must help us," Mandela had said famously in addressing the staff of Kruger. "You must bring us many foreign visitors and their money to South Africa."[102]

Around that time, the South Africa Tourist Board was expecting 1.8 million overseas visitors by the year 2000, with the tourists spending an average of about $1,500. The hope was that more than $2.5 billion would come into the country annually, helping not just the Steve Gibsons and Neville Edwardses, and the white motel and lodge operators, but black Africans in the townships who could work in the park's shops or run concessions.[103]

To help placate those who wanted land, the new government focused on "social ecology." Park business would be conducted with an eye toward involving those on the boundaries. Black African art and crafts would be sold in the Kruger camps. Contracts with vendors for food, for snacks, for supplies would support companies employing South African blacks or run by South African blacks. And finally, too, the glass ceiling suppressing the rise of black rangers into the higher ranks of the park would shatter.

So it was in that manner that Mandela saved the park and sought to serve his people.

But to change the immigration rules to protect the Mozambicans moving through the park? No, that was a political bridge too far. Unemployment in South Africa approached 40 percent. Only a few fringe groups spoke out for Mozambicans, pointing out that the immigration law was the one major policy carried over from the apartheid state. Everyone else, it seemed, viewed the Mozambicans as a cause of unemployment. There was no shortage of tales about Mozambicans being beaten by black South Africans. Some even were killed by mobs in antirefugee riots.

And there was another step not taken to protect Mozambicans: "dehabituating" the lions, causing them to be again fearful of humans. Why not? For one very good reason. Lions were good for business. In fact, in some cases man-eating lions were very good for business. Rangers note that a private game camp elsewhere in Africa lost a careless tourist to a lion a few years back and feared a slump in business. Instead, business boomed. "They wanted to know the place was real," said Steve Gibson. "Everyone was waiting for the camp to fold. Instead, business increased. It gave the place an authentic feel."

In fact, luxury safaris and ecotourist camps can be desirable investments throughout Africa, and foreigners with hard currency are there to be attracted. One study noted that "the value of prime privately owned wildlife habitat has increased by as much 2500% during the last twenty years."[104] According to the same study, a good ecotourism/game ranch operation could provide an 11 percent return on capital. Investments in cattle ranching? Only about 1 percent. If done right, ecotourism and game ranching was the future of this region of South Africa.[105] By the late 1990s, about five thousand game ranches and four thousand mixed game and livestock ranches had sprouted in South Africa. They covered about 13 percent of the country's land area versus only about 5.8 percent for official conservation areas. National parks cover only about 2.8 percent. Not all the game ranches were ecotourist operations, but the trend was there.[106]

But as natural as a land might be, it never was truly Africa—it never really was wild—without the big predators. As ex-Green Beret and grizzly bear lover Doug Peacock is fond of saying: "If there isn't something big enough and mean enough out there to eat you, then it's not really big wilderness."[107]

There was more to it than that, though. If you were looking to establish a wild place, then nature *needed* the lions to keep the wild

wild. If wilderness was a salable commodity, then wild lions were absolutely necessary, the yeast that made the wine. Modern zoologists would explain this need in complex terms of keystone species. The short, unscientific version was that an uber, apex, alpha, number one predator kept nature balanced.

"Lose the big predators," author David Quammen once wrote, "and there may come an overabundance of middle-sized predators, of herbivores, of seed predators—a pestilence of minor nibblers, cropping the vegetation down to stubs, interfering with tree reproduction, jeopardizing the long-term renewal of the forest canopy, exterminating populations of ground-nesting birds and probably of other small creatures as well."

This would be no small loss, and it extended beyond the touchy-feely. Commercially, only "natural" sold. In their presentation about the use of ranch land for nature preserves, "Reinventing the Commons," researchers David Schmidtz and Elizabeth Willott concluded: "Customers do not fly across the ocean for the experience of being in something that resembles a zoo. They want open space. They want their wildlife wild, not 'potted.' They want to see animals fending for themselves in a natural ecosystem, born to the land rather than stocked by owners. The kind of customer who flies to Africa tends to want reality, not the programmed experience of an amusement park."

Citizens of Marloth Park, the resort suburb community of Kruger, were for that exact reason concerned when lions crossed the river and attacked servants in their subdivision, not because of the danger to the servants but in part because of the danger that the lions would be *removed*, hurting property values and spoiling their enjoyment of homes truly in the wild.

"Take the lions away and this place is nothing," one landowner said. "Real estate prices will tumble." When Gerrie Camacho sought to dart and remove the lions, he was roundly booed.[108]

The ultimate reality and the ultimate value for the new ecotourist clearly is the ultimate African predator. No one truly felt fulfilled on an ecotourism trip unless lions were seen. It had been that way since Kruger started. Lions kept the customers coming. Lions were the rock stars that filled the stadium. A nature preserve without lions? It was a beach without an ocean.

And in fact what could be a better litmus test of wildness than lions eating, well, people? If lions were a draw, man-eating lions were an industrial-strength magnet. If wild lions sold seats in the park, man-eating lions could take the park platinum. Never was it marketed in such a manner, of course. But still, like "whisper figures" on Wall Street, the news was conveyed. You want to see real lions? Then get yourself to Kruger.

Against such a background the rangers now considered the fate of lions that killed humans. In the old days, even under James Stevenson-Hamilton, the savior of the lions, the response would be simple: find the lions, kill them. Even if it seemed the lion was only remotely guilty of attacking any human, black or white, the penalty was death. Such lion behavior was intolerable. Unnatural. Even the hint of man-eating was to be punished by quick death.

But over the years, values had changed. Rangers now devoted their lives to *preserving* wildlife. Their job was to save lions, not kill them. Most rangers worked in relatively low-paying jobs because they loved the work and loved nature. Shooting lions was not part of the deal.

And how could they kill the species that drew the tourists to the park and kept the natural world natural? Even to dehabituate the lions to humans—with flash-bang grenades or stun guns—would hurt business. The lions would avoid the roads. The tourists would not come in such numbers.

If that thought was kept quiet, others were not, particularly among the outspoken green public. An environmentally aware public was so concerned for animals that it gave the rangers few options in terms of culling—even if it seemed to be in the long-term favor of the animals. For example, Kruger was so crowded with elephants that trees, vegetation, and other species were suffering. The only true natural enemy of elephants is man, and in years past the rangers traditionally thinned herds on a regular basis.

The rangers would oversedate the elephants—a good deal tidier a death than elephants experienced in "natural" Africa. The white hunter George Rushby described one method pygmy tribes used in another part of Africa. They would isolate large herds of elephants in dry, grassy areas, twenty miles square, and, when the wind was right, drag smoking ropes of rushes through the dry grass. Elephants burned to death by the dozens.[109]

But even the modern-day methods brought protests and suits, and kept park rangers from culling the herds for years; now the elephant herds were destroying the habitat of other species and girdling the bark of the giant baobab trees. Some park officials estimated it would take forty years for the park to recover if Kruger's elephants were culled immediately.

And as for culling lions? Every time a "refugee-lion incident" was reported, the news brought as much sympathy for the lions as for the refugees.

Emotions were at play, but so were economics. Perhaps it was harsh and cynical to look at it this way, but protecting Mozambicans just did not make dollar and cents sense. Perhaps it was not cynical at all but merely impolite to mention because it was true—the crazy aunt thumping about in the attic that no one ever talked about happened to be a rich crazy aunt.

The underlying truth was that the average per capita earnings of a Mozambican was only about $300 to $400 a year, and the bottom tier most likely to migrate through Kruger could earn as little as $80 a year. The average Mozambican died at age forty-three. The lifetime economic earnings? Only about $12,000.

Black South Africans and white alike strongly favored tough immigration controls. It was said that a Mozambican would do anything for nothing. Moreover, it could be said with a slight degree of accuracy—at least in Marloth—that some crime came along for the ride with the refugees. The brutal murder of a Marloth radio celebrity shocked the community, and one Mozambican killed by a lion was said to have been stealing solar panels. And, yes, there were Mozambicans who poached.

A lion, on the other hand, was regarded as an object of value. A lion was said by some studies to be worth at least $120,000 in tourist revenue over the course of its ten-year lifetime, and a leopard in South Africa's Londolozi Game Reserve was said to bring in $50,000 annually in tourist dollars—a cool half million if the big cat lived a decade. And both of those figures were based on mid-1980 dollars.[110] They would be considerably higher today, postapartheid. Nearly doubled in fact.

Not everyone knew those figures, yet at some level everyone sensed them. Silently, they were there, present on the table in any discussion of the Mozambican problem.

As a result, a new covenant was forged between men and lions, and not all men and women and children came out well. In fact, the refugees were seen at the beginning of the new millennium as lions were at the beginning of the last century: of no use. As something that hurt the proper civilized world. As God-cursed. To be kept out of or driven from Eden.

The Mozambicans in short had become the new vermin, remarkably similar to the lions of 1902. The one subtle difference is that no one sets out to deliberately kill the refugees. No one sets out to save them either.

What is the price in human lives? Not the dollars, but the body count?

It appears almost certainly to be among the highest ever recorded, higher than Tsavo, higher than Tanganyika.

Continuing to try to answer that question, I walk a few hundred feet from the library in Skukuza to the office of Willelm Gertenbach. He says only one or two bodies are found each year, but in some years there have been many, many more. He is a precise man with a strict sense of order, one of the last of the Afrikaner scientists who have run the park post-Stevenson-Hamilton, and run it well. He makes it directly clear to me that I am one day late for our interview and such tardiness is not a desirable trait in a human halfway around the globe from wherever. Having taken care of that, he impassively moves on to the business at hand directly and forthrightly, no hard feelings.

Gertenbach in fact notes without prompting that the real number of deaths is almost certainly much higher than the bodies found. The tatters of clothes, shoes, and suitcases are seen on a regular basis, with no explanation and no bodies. Scavengers do not let protein or bones go untouched. Still, those biomass and scat studies—studies that could refine the guess—have not been undertaken. Of all the prey studied in the park, mankind is not one of them.

More research has been done, in fact, on the famous two man-eaters of Tsavo that roamed one hundred years ago. A whole industry of book publishing and academic research continues to this day on the Tsavo lions, called Ghost and Darkness by the Kenyans. But little is written anywhere, even in scientific papers, about Kruger man-eaters today.

It is not hard to understand and to sympathize with the scientists and rangers of Kruger. How do you research something that could reflect badly on the endangered species you are attempting to conserve? But how do you *not* research such a relatively rare phenomenon when it is also taking such a toll in human life? For whatever reasons, very little is known about the actual numbers. There is value in knowing how many ungulates are consumed by lions, and whether prides specialize in buffalo, giraffes, zebras, wildebeests, or impalas. Not so much value in compiling the consumption of humans.

Still, the compiling needs to be done. The deaths must be witnessed, if only through statistics. Or at least a step must be taken toward that goal.

From a "trophy" standpoint, I do not care whether Kruger National Park is the site of the largest incidence of man-eating lions in modern history or whether Tsavo or Tanganyika or Tanzania or Mozambique is. I simply do not have a dog in that catfight. I do care that so many have died in Kruger and that the cost in human lives is not widely known and the problem is far from solved.

So an estimate of the number of deaths is essential to this story for that reason—to bear witness. The comparison to the past records of famous man-eaters gives a useful reference point, and also some insight into how kills are counted.

Historically, two instances tower above all other past incidences of lions eating humans. First is the most famous, the man-eaters of Tsavo. Then come the less well-known but more deadly man-eaters of Tanganyika. It is said that nearly one hundred forty people were eaten near Tsavo and more than fifteen hundred were eaten in Tanganyika—the "All-Africa" record.

Before attempting to estimate the numbers killed in Kruger, it is worthwhile to examine the measurement techniques of the total of these two earlier kills. Truth is, the numbers of both stand on shaky ground. Most serious researchers believe Colonel Patterson could document just twenty-eight kills by the two famous man-eaters of Tsavo. The extra hundred or so seemed to grow from the retelling of the story and broad estimates of the numbers of unskilled African laborers killed. Yet only the skilled laborers on payroll were counted in that first estimate of twenty-eight.[111]

Certainly twenty-eight dead taken by two lions that shut down the construction of an entire railroad for months while an experienced hunter sought them out is dramatic. My guess is many other unskilled workers were dragged away as well and simply not counted. But the Tsavo killings were notable in the Western world more because of the economic consequences, Colonel Patterson's dogged pursuit, romantic newspaper stories about that pursuit, and his ability to write a good tale.

The Tanganyika All-Africa record of killings by lions is another story. It is little known because it happened in a more remote region and had little economic consequence to the Western world. From the late 1930s through the late 1940s, a large pride of lions is said to have specialized in humans and handed down that specialty from one generation to the next. It is unclear, upon examination of the literature, just how the number fifteen hundred was determined. It seems like a best guess of regional western government officials based on stories told by villagers, if you read the biography of George Rushby, the hunter who eventually killed the pride members after a three-year chase.[112] Again, there is no doubt that the pride claimed many humans—about one hundred fifty a year if the estimate is correct. But again, too, there is no firm and precise data to substantiate the exact number used in the estimate.

The point is not that fewer people were killed than claimed; the point is that exact estimates are tough to come by.

How to estimate the kills in Kruger then? In modern Tanzania in 2005, lion conservationist Craig Packer of the University of Minnesota was able to compile records based on the reports of police and of villagers who missed their husbands, wives, and children and were able to identify the remains.[113]

This is the gold standard for lion metrics. But in Kruger, that method does not work well. Mozambicans crossing the border illegally are not missed immediately if their intent is to cross and work in South Africa. If they are missed, the families do not inform the South African police that their husband, wife, daughter, or son illegally entered South Africa and now is missing.

Even for the anonymous bodies found, poor police records are kept. Efforts to obtain police files of famous cases outlined in newspaper articles resulted in the police saying they had no such record of any such case.

Another method of determining the consumption of humans in the park would be to conduct lion scat studies to determine human remains there. Such methods are used to estimate lion consumption of other animals—but not of humans.[114]

So where to begin? If I cannot build a number from the bottom up?

Take a top-down approach. If I can estimate the number of Mozambicans captured by the park and the total number moving through the park, I at least have a basis of suggesting how many may have been taken by lions.

Here are the knowns. The crackdown on Mozambicans began for real in the 1960s when the fight by native Mozambicans against the Portuguese colonial government began for real and the refugee tide rose significantly.[115] The crackdown forced the illegals to travel at night. Night travel brought the refugees in contact with lions and has now for more than forty-five years.

How many immigrants moved through the park? Park rangers and South African army patrols say they catch about four thousand refugees per year on average now out of an estimated total of sixteen thousand, and generally believe that for every one refugee they catch, three escape.[116] But in previous years the total numbers were much higher. Nearly fifty thousand were caught in 1995 and 1996 and the army projection then would place the total number of refugees moving through the park at around two hundred thousand, or one hundred thousand per year.[117]

It is estimated that the 1980s and the excess of a horrible civil war pushed more than three hundred fifty thousand immigrants through the park, or about thirty-five thousand per year.[118] The U.S. Committee for Refugees estimates that 1.7 million refugees were driven from Mozambique in the 1980s and 1990s—not all of them through Kruger, but a good many. Between 1990 and 1997, the South African government deported back to Mozambique about seven hundred forty thousand people—a bit more than one hundred thousand per year.[119] This is a significant number because many immigrants simply turn back around and trek through the park again, and the number syncs with the 1995 and 1996 reports of refugees captured and projections for totals in the park, giving substance to those numbers in the 1990s.

Press reports appear to suggest that only about two thousand were caught per year between 1960 and 1980 indicating a traffic through the park of about eight thousand per year over that twenty-year period, based on army estimates and ratios of captured to total number of refugees. Recent press reports suggest millions of refugees have crossed into South Africa, but most serious analysts discount those figures as a result of xenophobic passions among the press and unemployed South Africans.[120]

So, with all that top-down data merged, a scenario of Mozambique movement through the park might reasonably look like this.

    1960 to 1980—8,000 per year or 160,000 total
    1980 to 1990—35,000 per year or 350,000 total
    1990 to 1997—100,000 per year or 700,000 total
    1997 to 2005—16,000 per year or 128,000 total

Rangers and the army patrols estimate they catch about 25 percent of those who cross. Lions, far better equipped and incentivized to detect the refugees, could, one might think, catch at least that many.

But other factors do come into play. Some immigrants will be "lion smart" and know to make a stand rather than run. Some lions may indeed be spooked by humans and just not look on them as food, even opportunistically. There is an abundance of ungulates in the park, after all. Still other lions will not see trigger signals and will not attack. Moreover, perhaps the rangers catch the slowest-of-foot-and-mind refugees near the border before the lions do and only the more skilled immigrants, with better survival skills, encounter lions later and are better equipped to evade harm.

So assume for the moment that lions do not catch as many immigrants as the rangers and army patrols.

On the other side of the lion ledger are these facts. We do know from press and park reports that lions have killed refugees regularly over a period of years dating from 1898, and that in the war and famine years immigrants literally stumbled through the park—walking trigger points for opportunistic lions on the hunt.[121] The law of "easy prey" will often apply. Whether the lions prefer antelope, zebras, buffalo, or giraffes, a sick refugee stumbled upon will do nicely. We know too that at least some lions are not opportunistic killers but according to credible rangers display a preference for and specialty for humans, waiting along the power lines.[122] We do know that the lions have been habituated to humans for more than a century. We know they see six times better than humans at night.

But let's say the lions do not catch nearly as many refugees as government officials do. Let's say in fact that they catch only 1 percent of all refugees—performing twenty-five times worse than the rangers and army patrols.

At that rate of 1 percent, then the lions of Kruger have killed and consumed about 13,380 Mozambicans.[123]

Estimates of Refugee Traffic and Lion Kills of Refugees at 1 Percent Rate

	Ranger apprehension	Total crossing	Fatalities if 1 percent claimed by lions
1960–1980	40,000	160,000	1,600
1980–1990	85,000	350,000	3,500
1990–1997	175,000	700,000	7,000
1997–2005	70,000	128,000	1,280
Total		1,338,000	
Total fatalities			13,380

Is that the new All-Africa record? It depends on your point of view, of course. The "score" for Kruger lions is racked up by many lions—not just one pride—over many decades, not just one as in Tanganyika, or less than a year in the case of Tsavo.

But from 1960 through 2005, I think it fair odds that the lions of Kruger attacked and killed more than the Tanganyika lions and the Tsavo lions combined.

Is the estimate flawed and exaggerated? Gertenbech thinks it might be. But if the 1 percent estimate is halved, this "record" still holds true at around 6,650 dead. And if the 0.50 percent is halved again to one-quarter of 1 percent, the tally at around 3,325 still beats the other famous kills. Halve the 0.25 percent and state that only about one-eighth of 1 percent of all refugees are taken by lions and the number still beats Tanganyika and Tsavo combined at around 1,650.

In total, even the one-eighth of 1 percent number results in so many deaths of humans that the All-Africa record seems very sadly beside the point.

Some scientists I have spoken to say the top-down approach paints a picture with a too-broad brush. Others agree the four thousand refugees captured each year by rangers is a good starting point for estimating the biomass of potential human prey—the density of prey mass to land area. Gnoske and Peterhans use a similar method to estimate slave deaths in the caravans of the nineteenth century. The top-down analysis of the four thousand refugees captured provides, at least, a basis to compute exposure to risk. And the conservative numbers I use, they say, are not a bad way to at least frame the question for debate. To at least explore the new paradigm.

Gerrie Camacho feels strongly that my numbers are conservative and that a 1 percent extrapolation understates the total number of kills by many factors. He is a scientist, but he has trouble with the current techniques of scientific measurement of animals killing humans. Data is the basis of many scientific assumptions, but often the data is flawed.

"They say that the hippo is the largest killer of humans in Africa," Camacho said in an interview. "I would question that. The hippo is just the most obvious killer, because it leaves bodies behind. It kills people when they get between the hippo and the water or otherwise upset the hippo, but it does not eat the people. When a lion, or a crocodile for that matter, kills a human, nothing is left.

"I doubt seriously that hippos kill more humans than lions; hippos just leave more bodies behind. And science only considers what it can measure. It does not account for those people who go down to the river but never come back because they are eaten and consumed entirely by crocodiles, and there are dozens and dozens and dozens of those stories. It does not measure the person who goes out for wood and is killed and eaten by a lion and then scavenged by hyenas, jackals, and vultures. There is nothing to count. And believe me, there are many, many people who just disappear, so far as science is concerned for no reason at all."

Regardless of the exact number, the seriousness of the Kruger problem over the past four decades is not open to debate. Mozambicans have been eaten by lions in Kruger in very large numbers for the past four decades, and in total this death toll almost certainly ranks as one of the largest lion kills of humans in any place at any time of recorded modern history.

And while the notion of such a tragedy is well known among park officials and conservationists, they have done little to halt the loss of human life.

The scholarship of the scientists of Kruger is beyond question. The tradition of Kruger's conservation mission is secure. The book *The Kruger Experience—Ecology and Management of Savanna Heterogeneity*, establishes this within its 516 pages. Read it cover to cover and you'll learn of the fascinating play of biotic and abiotic factors that help create heterogeneity, and of an intriguing record of one hundred years of experimentation in conservation. The Kruger scientists acknowledge mistakes and correct them. But nowhere in those pages is there a discussion or mention of the clearly established pattern of man-eating behavior that has existed for at least three decades.

There is little hope that the scientists will come up with a solution to a problem that is not acknowledged. Proposals from other sectors are elusive and ill defined, other than for "things to get better in Mozambique" or for the lions to somehow just stop. The Mozambican economy is improving, it is said, but unlikely to dim the attraction of South African jobs. And the lions are never likely to lose an appetite for easy prey. In any event, park officials can do little. "We are not equipped to solve this problem," Gertenbach said. "We are short-handed now in performing our major functions—patrolling for poachers and snares, fighting fires, and maintaining the park for the animals and the tourists."

Which is not to say Gertenbach does not care about the refugees. He has tried. He suggested that buses be set up on the border and visas issued. But the South African Department of Home Affairs thought otherwise. As in America, a substantial portion of the South African population views the immigrants as border jumpers who steal jobs. To some, the lions are just a sort of biological razor wire, a way to literally put teeth into the border patrol efforts. The immigrants are perceived as work thieves. Nevertheless, the demand for labor in South African mines and ranches and farms and factories creates a powerful osmosis that draws the immigrants through porous borders as it has for more than a century. The plagues and politics and famines push the immigrants just as powerfully. And so the migration of a prey species continues.

In addition, officials once proposed a barter trade with Mozambicans along the border. They would provide crafts, the park would sell them in the shops. They would give the potential refugees food, and they would stay in their home country. New park vendors did not like the suggestion, and it never came to be.

On a continent where more than 40 million people are infected with AIDS, where genocide by machete cuts down hundreds of thousands, where malaria still claims hundreds of thousands in South Africa alone, the lion deaths do not command the prime focus of the outside world. Nor are they likely to. Nor, perhaps, in the context of so many other deaths, should Bono or Bill and Melinda Gates change their work from AIDS and malaria relief to the plight of Mozambican refugees.

But surely someone must.

Surely some deaths are symbolically more important than others. Mosquitoes can be deadly—but not predators for whom humans are meat. Do wild animals eat humans with impunity? Is that not an ultimate threshold question to measure civilization? If one dips a litmus strip into that beaker, what ugly color does it turn? If such an obvious matter is not recognized and treated, can the more abstract issues of malaria and AIDS be?

Gertenbach is not optimistic. The Mozambicans have lousy PR. Their famines are not fashionable. No celebrities are present, no visuals on the BBC or NBC. As to their crossing Kruger, the jackals, the vultures, the hyenas destroy so much of the evidence that even a CSI crew could not reconstruct the crimes here.

One Kruger ranger feels that even rains and food and economic improvement in Mozambique would not stop the migrations. "You cannot just do nothing and die, just starve, but even if conditions get better, you will have families and tribes, people related to each other, split by the park," he said. "They will always cross. Yes, they will always cross."

Certainly, the refugees will be taking that hike. Yes, the situation in Mozambique has stabilized some. But no, the problems are not over. Always, there seems to be a problem. A horrible flood in 2000. Then a horrible drought. "With this dryness, if the drought continues, I would expect there would be even more refugees," Gertenbach said.

He is a man of science, and a good man, but he too could not find where the puzzle pieces fit, and in the end, try as he might, he could not slay the monster either.

Chapter 10

LION POLITICS AND JUSTICE

Even where some mammals are more equal than others, some lions are killed; the honor and dignity of the pursuit of man-eaters is a thing of the past; a hunt described.

Steve Gibson and Neville Edwards knew they were back in touch with their old bush lives one day in 1992 while on a week's hunting safari in South Africa. They drove an old Willys Jeep—almost the same as the old World War II American model, with rugged four-wheel drive but not much engine under the hood.

Their tracker was a man who responded to questions only in Zulu, not English, which posed no problem since Steve and Neville were both fluent in the language.

"During our hunt, we would take turns in hunting, and the other driving," Neville recalled. "This one particular day, Steve was shooting and set off with the tracker on foot when we had spotted animals.

"I stayed behind with the vehicle until they returned. Whilst they were out, and just before they returned, I spotted a white male rhino down the road on the beaten track going down toward a dry riverbed."

They asked the tracker if it would be safe to continue toward the rhino. After some discussion, all agreed that it would, that the rhino posed no threat.

"With me driving, the tracker directly behind me, and Steve next to me, we set off, only to find that there was a second rhino, female," Neville explained. "What we never realized was they had been copulating or were attempting to copulate, and visitors were out of bounds."

The male retreated into the bush, but as the old Jeep slowly passed, the rhino wound itself up and charged in a galloping fury.

"Put your foot down! Go, go, go!" Steve said. But the old Willys Jeep could reach only sixty kilometers per hour with a tailwind. Neville turned the Jeep downhill. This helped the Jeep accelerate, but also helped the rhino.

"When I peeped to the right the rhino was there at my side," Neville said. At the same time, the Jeep was approaching the dry riverbed. The animal banged against the vehicle on Neville's side. Steve was shouting "go, go, go!" and hanging onto the weapons as Neville was torn between going faster or braking for the abrupt end of the downhill road at the dry riverbed. The tracker too was yelling emphatically in Zulu.

"At that moment the Zulu tracker decided that he could speak English," Neville said, "as maybe we would not understand what he was shouting in Zulu, which we knew was 'fuck go, go, go, fuck, fuck, fuck, go!'

"The tracker took off his hat and belted the rhino as the rhino belted the jeep and said in perfectly enunciated English, 'Faster, sir, faster, sir! We need more, faster!"

The rhino took one last swipe at the Jeep and peeled away; it had established a comfort zone and returned to its mate. Steve, Neville, and the tracker all felt better now, except they were hurtling toward the dry creek bed at more than seventy kilometers and the Jeep's capacity for deceleration was even worse than its capacity for acceleration. Neville pumped the brakes and finally felt them engage, but by then it was too late.

"We hit the riverbed at top speed with a tremendous thump and a jolt, sand flying everywhere," Neville said. "The impact slowed us, but we flew out the other side of the riverbed and up the road for another half kilometer or so before we could stop.

"There we stopped; we looked at one another, and I said to Steve, 'You OK?'"

"Yeah," said Steve, who smiled from ear to ear and added, "God, but that was great! Should we do it again?"

Clearly, they had established themselves in a new home. They had great credentials for resettlement, of course. They were skilled in the bush, intelligent, and, at a time when it was very important, white. This gave them open border crossings and first-class status in apartheid South Africa. Yes, they worked hard. But yes, the political, economic, and racial stars were aligned in their favor.

By contrast, Mozambicans trying to get to South Africa were not only illegal immigrants, they were often victimized even if they did manage to cross the Kruger and find work. The Mozambicans, like Steve and Neville, often are driven from their country, and are sometimes very welcomed by those looking for cheap labor. Like John, some settle in a pattern that parallels the resettlement of Steve and Neville.

But the resettlement of a refugee can change at a moment. An employer who wanted to save money simply blew the whistle a day before payday and the refugee was headed back to Mozambique minus a paycheck. There was no justice, no appeal, just a train trip home.

And then there are the lions. Even though it may seem at times as if lions rank higher in social status than refugees, lions who have run-ins with Mozambicans can be victims, too. It happens infrequently, but sometimes the lions lose. There is retribution and "lion justice"—though it seems pointless and severely unjust to many.

In fact, the whole problem of the lions and the refugees has been regarded not so much as one of immigration and settlement but as "lion control" and refugee deportation. And while the refugees seem to have gotten by far the shorter end of the stick, the lions also get caught up in the conflicts.

Intentional killings of lions are rare. Steve and Neville have heard of only one incident where lions paid with their lives for eating humans, and Neville for one did not consider it justice at all. "It was tourist politics," he said without judgment. "They felt they had to show they were doing something, so they picked one pride and killed it."

Later I turn up at least two more cases of lions being shot, but both were caught literally in the act of eating a human carcass. Despite the few incidents, lions do pay a price.

"Some people say, well, the lions were here first, and man comes in and creates a problem, so why must the animal suffer," said Gertenbach. "That is a difficult statement to make. There *are* human rights."

But only the most horrible incidents seem to provoke that concern. In 1997, five refugees had huddled around a fire designed to keep them warm and ward off lions. This was in the vicinity of the notorious Punda Maria pride.

The men heard lion roars nearby, then piled on more wood to make the fire larger. Some myths about lions are true. Some are not. One myth is that lions fear fire. But it depends on the lion, and it depends on the fire.[124]

The fire meant little to the Punda pride. One lion charged into the group and took a man down. The four survivors fled to a tree. It is another myth that lions will not climb trees. Sometimes they do; sometimes they don't. In this case, the Punda pride simply scrambled up the tree after the men and dragged three of them down. Only the man in the topmost branches survived.

"They had become too aggressive," Gertenbach said of these lions. "We could tell they were confirmed man-eaters. In one stomach, we found a wallet with Mozambique currency. Said a park ranger on the excursion, "Next, we would have been their targets. Even though we were fully armed, when we were in the bush, they were watching us and waiting, and they had become very aggressive."

And here a small skirmish line forms in the lion information wars. "This, I think, is more rationalization than fact," Camacho said of this incident. "Confront a lion on its kill? Yes, it will look at you funny. Does that make it a man-eater? I do not think so. I think it is something someone says when they do not really want to kill a lion but need to rationalize it."

But rangers on that trip describe a different sort of lion-man relationship. Before the darts flew, a park veterinarian stepped out of his vehicle to test the temperament of the pride. Although they had abundant zebras in front of them, one lioness left the kill and advanced toward the man with keen interest.[125]

In another case, park veterinarian Douw Grobler described in *African Lion News* how lions seemed to stake out the Caborra Bassa power lines and "were responsible for killing and eating several illegal immigrants. . . . this group stayed close to the Klopperfontein water-hole and even tried to attack some . . . field staff whilst patrolling the area by bicycle.

"On the previous Friday afternoon . . . personnel went shopping and one of the lionesses almost took a person off the back of the open truck," he continued.

The staff decided that this pride needed to be taken down as well, so the lions were called to a zebra carcass as the rangers waited to dart them from a position some thirty meters away.

"I stepped out of the vehicle to check their reaction: normal lions would scatter immediately, but these lions saw it as an opportunity to supplement their zebra meat and approached me immediately," Grobler wrote. "My hair stood on end seeing the stare especially from the male and we proceeded to euthanize these lions. It was a gross sight dealing with the necropsies of these lions afterwards as they were filled with human remains, clothing with ID book and purse still intact."[126]

Tourist politics or justice for man-eaters, the executions are isolated and there is no current death row for the lions, no intense focus on killing lions out of retribution. The lions are the main draw of the park, for one thing, the stars of the show. But for another, Camacho and others seem to have won the information wars for now. No one really *blames* the lions and in fact, the laws of lion justice are loosely written and enforced even more loosely. There is that sense of don't ask, don't tell.

"When we know clearly that a lion has become a man-eater, then we must shoot it," Gertenbach said. "We are guided by the behavior of the animal and if you see that they have lost fear. But if it is not clear, if it is not absolutely clear, we give it the benefit of the doubt." Others say quietly that if tough tests were applied, very few of the lion prides, particularly in the north, would pass. For they may not be man-eaters, but many, many of them in the northern prides have eaten men and women and children as opportunity presented.

For those lions deemed man-eaters, rangers set out to find them and use lethal force.

The lore of the great white hunter tracking down man-eaters in Africa and India has consumed whole library shelves. The most famous African hunter, of course, is John H. Patterson, the good British colonel who sought to build a bridge in Tsavo, only to have two lions—Ghost and Darkness—bring the whole project to a halt. Two movies were made based on the saga—one a cheese-ball 3-D 1950s' thriller, the other a more contemplative effort with a William Goldman script. Dozens of books, papers, and theses have been written since and more are on the way.

Patterson was an experienced hunter and tried everything he knew. He sat in trees over bait. He concocted a trap for the lions. He and the workers built thorn enclosures and fed huge fires at night.

But the two lions worked the encampments as clever house cats might work a mouse colony. They struck in different spots on different nights, never in the same place twice. If Patterson sat up over bait to the north, they were in the south. When he went south, they went east. They crept through the *nyika*, the vast thorn bush maze, then into tents and grabbed workers by the head and rushed them off into the thorny bush.

It was only through luck and grit that Patterson shot first one and then the other, both within a few weeks. The last lion was so determined to kill Patterson before Patterson killed it that the lion took six shots from a heavy-caliber rifle. At the last, with a crippled leg, it was still crawling toward Patterson, biting sticks and grass, ever focused on its prey.[127]

The case in Tanganyika—now called Tanzania—was less famous but far more of a mess. A pride functioned effectively for nearly ten years through two or three generations of lions between 1938 and 1947 before George Rushby finally hunted down the lions. They, too, had perfected a technique. They would enter a village casually, choose a house, claw through the grass thatching, and select one or two of the inhabitants. They would then race with the victim into the bush and by relays take the corpse some miles away before eating. Rushby would go to the last village, but the lions would be at the next, striking fifteen miles away in a different and unpredictable region.

The local people were convinced it was *muti*, magic, men reincarnated as lions to punish them, or paid to wreak evil and carnage. Some simply abandoned villages to the lions and left. Rushby took more than a year to catch up with the first of the pride, and when he killed the first one, what he found frightened him. These were healthy specimens with excellent, slick coats, good teeth, and sound, strong legs. These were no old or lame lions, as had been rumored, but animals at the peak of their game.

He would get one here, one there, through traps and poisons and direct confrontations at times. But only after two years of hunting did he kill the fifteenth lion. Only then was there a noticeable drop-off in the number of human deaths. Rushby was the hero of the time, though some said the killings stopped only after a local healer took away the curse.[128]

Kruger had its own heroes, of course, and when it came to killers of the great cats, there was no shortage at all, black or white. A famous character of Kruger lore was the legendary Mubi, an African who would alternate between poaching and policing. Once, in the 1930s, he passed by one of the few villages left in the reserve. The women complained that a leopard had been stealing goats and was holed up in a thicket only a few hundred feet away. When Mubi ignored the women, they laughed at him and said the great Mubi was afraid. They dared him to kill the leopard.

A leopard, cornered, is the nightmare of any big game hunter, even if armed to the teeth. Capstick tells a story of a wounded leopard that clawed and hospitalized three successive well-armed white hunters who were bound by the code of their profession to dispatch animals wounded by clients.

Unlike lions, leopards do not announce their charge with grunts and coughs. They stalk and attack silently from ambush. Capstick himself would consider pursuing a wounded leopard only after donning a leather Marine Corp fencing guard for his neck, various pieces of body armor, heavy clothing, and a short-barreled pump shotgun of the type used by riot policemen breaking down the doors of armed suspects.[129]

Mubi looked at the laughing women, called to his small dog, and strode toward the overgrown area and the leopard, armed only with a short stabbing spear called an assegai. Dog and hunter disappeared. A commotion followed in the brush. Birds flew up. Fifteen minutes later, Mubi walked out dragging the dead leopard by the tail. He dropped the animal without comment and continued on his previous route, the little dog at his heels. The leopard had charged, and Mubi had so coolly and competently speared it through the heart that he was completely unmarked.[130]

There also came a time in the 1920s when a seasoned African ranger named Mafuta tracked a wounded lion that was said to have threatened workers in Kruger. There was a confrontation. The lion charged. Mafuta fired his rifle. The lion came forward, unstopped. Mafuta, unable to reload the single-shot rifle quickly enough, ran for a tree. He was well off the ground when the lion jumped up and caught him. As the lion pulled him down, the ranger reached for his knife. Lion and man rolled in the dust, each attempting to gain advantage, the lion fixed to Mafuta's thigh, the ranger sticking the lion wherever he could.

Finally, the lion went limp on top of Mafuta. He slid out from under the animal, leaving his knife impaled in the creature's breast. The ranger bound up his terrible wounds and walked for a while, but knew he could not make it. He rested beneath a tree, did what he could for the horrible damage to his thigh. The femoral artery had been chewed through. No one survives that without immediate medical help. He moved once to get out of the sun, fixed his eyes on the far horizon. They found him dead the next morning.[131]

Then there was the hired gun whom Stevenson-Hamilton employed in 1925—a time when anti-lion agitation threatened the future of the park. Conservationists joined with ranchers to demand that more lions be culled. Other reserves were folding up under the pressure.

"It was clear . . . that the lion menace did really form so genuine an excuse for agitation against the Reserve," Stevenson-Hamilton wrote, "that some drastic step should be taken to remove it, especially at this crucial period when the whole future of wild life preservation seemed to be in the melting-pot."[132]

The "drastic step" was the securing of the services of Harold Trollope. He was a dead shot and a hunter of great skill. But his actions went beyond that and perhaps of sanity itself. At first Trollope eliminated the lions near the Crocodile River, at the southern edge of the park, thus satisfying the immediate complaints of the ranchers. And then he started on other sections of the park, beyond his charter.[133]

It was as much the method by which he killed lions as the number he killed that made him famous—and made some wonder if he was all there. Simply eliminating lions was no great task if they were hunted down on horseback with a pack of good dogs. Lions tire quickly over distances and, winded, could be easily killed with little danger to the shooters. Or lions could be shot over bait, never knowing what hit them, if the shooter was good. Generally, lion hunters were more exterminators than sportsmen. The men traveled in packs with dogs and horses, and if one shot went astray, a volley would follow and bring the lion down.

The ease with which lions can be killed is deceiving. Caputo in *Ghosts of Tsavo* illustrated that in his contemporary case study of Brian Heath, a reluctant exterminator of lions who wandered off the Tsavo National Park on to the Galana Ranch, a huge, 1.6-million-acre enterprise just east of the park, which now raises cattle.

He has killed more than four hundred lions. When lions killed a cow, he would simply cover the carcass with canvas to keep away scavengers and other knackers of the wild, then lay up in a blind twenty-five to thirty yards away. With a scoped .375 H&H and a spotlight, Heath and a tracker would wait. They simply turned on the light when the lions came, around nine or ten of a night. The spot froze the lion enough for Heath to squeeze off a shot. The lions went down as if struck by a slaughterhouse bolt.

He could easily kill two lions in sequence in this manner with two shots, but often could not manage a third lion. If the third escaped, he and the tracker would simply wait until the heat of the next day, track the lion to the bush were it had holed up, and shoot the animal as it slept. He acknowledged the unsporting nature of the process and his distaste for it, but his job was to minimize risk and maximize kills. The sport of hunting was taken out of the equation when Kenya outlawed hunting in the mid-1970s, he told Caputo, which resulted in an upsurge of cattle-killing lions on Galana and the necessity of his position.[134] What killed the lions, he implies, was the ban on hunting that ended the economic underpinning for the existence of lions on Galana. Once lions could not produce revenue through hunting, they were viewed only as cattle killers. Well-meaning conservationists and the unintended consequences of their policies killed the lions, he seems to say. He simply pulled the trigger.

Trollope began the same way—as an executioner. He would gallop after lions and bring them to bay, just as the others did, or shoot them over bait.

But then he began going out alone. He stopped shooting over bait. Then after cornering a lion, he began waiting for the lion to recover its strength. And as this trend led to its illogical conclusion, Trollope would "go out of his way deliberately to invite charges," Stevenson-Hamilton wrote, "finding the sport not sufficiently exciting enough otherwise."[135]

Stevenson-Hamilton considered it beyond foolishness. An exhausted lion or a lion caught unaware could easily be killed with one well-placed round. But the literature of lion hunting is filled with stories of what happens when a lion is wounded or cornered and then charges. Even Brian Heath agrees with that. ". . . if you wounded him, you had real trouble. You don't want to botch it. It's very important to get your lion the first time."[136]

Peter Capstick catalogued the dangers of a charging wounded lion in one of his epic hunting books.

> First among them is his inclination to charge from close quarters where only a brain or spine shot will anchor him. You may blow a hole in his heart big enough to accommodate a navel orange, but in his condition of hyperadrenia, there will still be enough oxygen in his brain to carry his charge for a surprising distance and enough moxie left over to turn you into something that would give a hyena the dry heaves.
>
> The second factor . . . is the combination of his speed and strength and the small target he offers in a frontal charge. . . . In times of stress their movements are virtually nothing but blurs, a very unnerving fact at a time when you yourself are probably scared witless. A typical charge by a lion from sixty feet takes a blinking of an eye. . . . The average shot will be about fifteen yards. . . . At such a short range it is impossible to overestimate the degree of danger a hunter is subjected to. A lion can cover forty five feet quicker than you can pronounce it.[137]

Add to that the deceiving target of the lion's head. There is very little skull or brain above the lion's brow, Capstick noted, "just a mass of fatty tissue and mane."[138] Yet the instinct of a hunter seeking a brain shot is to shoot into this area, thinking he has the head well targeted when actually he may just be combing a new part into the lion's mane.

Lions have always been indiscriminate in their attacks, without consideration for royalty or race, title or class. Sir George Grey, the brother of a prime minister of Great Britain, took the charge of a lion in the early twentieth century. He stood solidly and his shots were well placed and hit the lion in the chest, but the lion killed him nonetheless.

Some speculate that Grey's fatal mistake might have been to use too little gun—a small .280 Ross high-velocity rifle. It was common among sportsmen then to hunt large game with what Robert Ruark called "souped up .22s"—a practice he decried in his book *Use Enough Gun*. The .280 carried a wallop from its velocity, but the bullet itself had little mass. Moreover, Sir George appears to have had no backup shooters to protect against the charge.

Then again, the smaller high-velocity rifles commonly kill lions at long range and Ruark himself was a self-confessed lousy shot with his. Moreover, "using enough gun" does not explain what happened on a Kenyan safari in 1967. Hunter and author Brian Herne chronicled the series of events in his book *White Hunters*. Veteran guide and hunter Henry Poolman took an experienced client out looking for the "big five"—lion, leopard, buffalo, elephant, and rhino. Pete Barrett, the client, was a crack shot and experienced hunter. Both men packed formidable weapons: a .458 Winchester for Barrett, a .470 double rifle for Poolman. Either weapon could take down an elephant, and in fact the men often were looking for elephant. Guides and bearers and scouts also carried a mix of weaponry, including a shotgun and a 7 mm rifle—the smaller bore, high-velocity rifle preferred for lion at a distance.

They came upon a lion at relatively close range, and Barrett let loose with a 510-grain bullet—nearly four times heavier than Ross's little 140 grain. The big cat ran as Barrett fired, however, and they thought he had missed. Then, when they topped a ridge, they saw the cat lying dead.

"Congratulations!" Poolman said to Barrett, and at the sound of a human voice, the "dead" lion rose and charged Barrett.

Poolman then did what the white hunter code called for. He placed himself between the lion and his client, and, as the lion was upon him, blasted away with both barrels of his elephant gun, squarely striking the lion with both shots.

The point-blank impact of an elephant gun slowed the lion hardly at all. It bowled over Poolman but did not harm him. The lion was after Pete Barrett. He caught up with the client, threw him to the ground, and mauled him. Barrett gave the lion one arm and attempted to fend the lion off with the other.

Poolman could not find his rifle, lost during the charge, but came to Barrett's aid bare-handed. He pulled the lion's tail, attempting to deflect its focus on Barrett. Meanwhile, one of Poolman's experienced gun bearers rushed forward with a 7 mm rifle and put three slugs expertly through the lion's heart and lungs as quickly as he could work the bolt of the rifle.

The lion reacted not at all and, shot through now with five slugs, continued to maul Barrett. In the confusion, an inexperienced gun bearer took aim at the lion's head as Poolman continued to pull on the animal's tail. The 12-gauge buckshot missed the lion, perhaps because of the disorienting nature of the mane. But the buckshot struck Poolman fully in the chest, killing him instantly.

Just moments later, the bullet-riddled lion simply stopped and rolled off Barrett, quite dead. The client survived the mauling, perhaps because Poolman's first shots had broken its lower jaw.

Hunter and author Herne's take on lions? "If the first shot is not well placed on a lion, it will trigger a swift adrenaline response. There is little question subsequent body shots are, for the time being at least, going to do very little to slow him down. If that first shot is not immediately fatal, the lion may quickly become the most formidable terrestrial animal on earth."[139]

It was this sort of danger Trollope courted, sometimes several times a day. He *forced* the charge. On every hunt, he bet that he could place a bullet at exactly the right spot in the lion's head or spine to stop a charge that a heart shot would not.

Was Trollope a sportsman or a bit touched? The other rangers thought some of both, but there was no doubt about one thing. He was a dead shot, and no lion laid tooth or claw upon him. Sometimes they would fall within feet of him. But he never was mauled or injured. He devastated the lion population in the 1920s, killing more than four hundred of them, until he tired of the sport and moved on.[140]

It seems appalling in this day and age. But Trollope gave Stevenson-Hamilton enough political capital to quell the anti-lion sentiment. Elsewhere in South Africa, preserves were reverting to the ranchers and farmers. But not the Sabi Reserve. And if nothing else could be said of Trollope, these two points surely could: he gave the lion a chance, and once Trollope passed through an area, no one suggested Stevenson-Hamilton and the reserve rangers were soft on lions. This fact may have been key to Stevenson-Hamilton's success in converting the reserve to a national park, where the lions were no longer culled.

But when it happens today, the killing of lions has none of the glory attached to it as in the days of the great white hunter. There is no ethic of fair pursuit. These are not brave sorties into the bush after fleeing demons. No Patterson at Tsavo. No Rushby in Tanganyika. No Hemingway or Ruark, with their immense but fragile egos, plucky wives, and witty safari sundowner banter. No Corbett chasing serial killer tigers in India. No noble Sir George Grey with his high-velocity little gun. No brave Poolman. No guts. Above all, no glory. Not even rifle shots mark these events.

Of the old days, Capstick said, "The brazen dedication of the experienced man-eating lion to his art can be spine-chilling. Just as a normal lion learns techniques of killing and hunting animal prey in specific manners, so does the man-eater develop modus operandi for catching humans. The fact that a man-eating feline is the most difficult animal in the world to hunt can be explained by the cat's ability to learn well and quickly."[141]

The truth today is that while the lions of Kruger are some of the deadliest in all of modern history, they are the least dangerous to kill. They are habituated to humans and simply do not fear them. The lions of Tsavo, of Tanganyika, knew humans as a foe and were in fact ferociously aggressive and cunningly elusive. The lions of Kruger know humans as slightly more dim-witted than warthogs and a lot easier to catch. Why run from a human? Or a Landie filled with rangers and their dart guns?

These are executions of stationary lions who never have felt the slightest need to flee from humans. In fact, they have been encouraged to tolerate cars filled with humans—else there is no show for the tourists.

When rangers took down the Punda pride in 1997, it was a relatively simple matter. Stake out a ripe zebra. Let the pride assemble. Pull alongside the carcass and the pride with a truck full of rangers and dart guns. Load the darts with lethal doses. The pride looks up curiously. There is a series of "pfffts"—a volley of air-rifle shots. Darts lob through the air. The lions swat or gnaw at the darts, stand up, walk a few wobbly steps, and then fall to the ground and die.[142]

The rangers who perform these missions are not happy, and the roots of their despair have little to do with the economics of anything or distaste for refugees.

They are caught in an existential riddle that no one can solve. This is a postmodern version of "The Lady or the Tiger?" Which do you choose? The lions or the refugees? Either choice has a horrible consequence for the chooser.

And it never is an easy choice for the rangers. All economics aside, their lives are built on a respect of nature and animal life, but they revere human life as well. They are intelligent people who have forsaken better-paying jobs and the comfort of cities for the work they love. They are the priests and priestesses of the park, men and women of honor.

But where is honor here?

Where is the honor in executing lions that are guilty of nothing but acting like lions? Smuts concluded in his studies that culling lions was like taking a bucket of water from a pool: the empty space was immediately filled.[143] The "easy prey" was still walking the power lines. The new lions would learn soon enough.

And where is the honor in letting that happen? Letting the refugees walk to certain death?

None at all, I conclude, and the situation seems hopeless. There simply is nothing the rangers can do. There was no great white hunter to solve this problem and slay the monster.

And of course, I could not have been more wrong and at the same time right.

The great hunter was not white, and the monster of a system was vulnerable after all.

Chapter 11

MACHABA'S WAY:
EAST FROM EDEN

We meet the Beowulf of Satara; the problem of birds and "nature" in general; a gentle encounter with tourists; a fitful night under the stars; a bold and unconventional approach

Over time, I am wearing down Neville's defenses on what the word *Nango*! means. He was not hiding some exotic profanity or secret exchange between the two men, he says, but he was puzzled about how to explain to a Yank a Zulu word used since childhood.

"It is so me and Steve? Depends on the type of conversation, or how it was concluded? I do believe it may be *nango, easy job*, meaning if we were hunting like we have done and you have had an excellent shot, *nango* would be more or less *there, you see*, followed by *easy job*, and later followed by whiskey and beers."

There has been no shortage of times at the end of the day when Neville punches Steve's now-bruised and numb left arm, and we all go for whiskey and beers. So I take it as a compliment that our safari is working as well for them as it is for me.

It is on a break from Neville and Steve that I meet up with a park official who has a quite unofficial manner of approaching the lion-refugee problem, and I get a nango moment of my own, with no one's arm to punch who would not punch back. I see him in action before I actually get to know him, and he seems the least probable of Beowulfs as he talks outside the concession area of Skukuza, one of the main Kruger encampments and one of the most popular.

"Oh, no, no, no, no, no, no, we could not do that, you see," Albert Machaba tells the white woman. His voice is a sweet lilt, musical, almost a coo. The tone tells the woman he is sympathetic, regretful, respectful. Unmistakably there is also an underlying presence of authority and principle.

The woman, white, in her thirties, runs the snack and dining concessions at the large tourist camp. Just a few years ago she would not have been asking Machaba or anyone with skin of color for permission to do anything at Kruger. She would have been talking to white managers.

But apartheid had fallen in '94. Machaba had studied hard earlier, spent four years in a South African college for wildlife conservation, joined the Kruger staff, and earned his stripes in the bush and a reputation as a crack shot with a rifle when he needed to be. Now, in his forties, he is the chief ranger for the entire Satara District of Kruger, a large expanse of bushveld that covers the central third of the great park.

And now she needs to come to him if she wants something, and, it has to be said, she does not seem to resent it and is not condescending. She simply wants the birds kept away from the outside dining areas near the snack bar. But she cannot do that, and Machaba is explaining why.

"If we built screens, you see, it would intrude upon nature," Machaba continues. He wears the dark green epauletted sweater of the Kruger rangers, along with crisp khaki pants—the uniform of senior field management.

"And that is what we cannot do in the park, we cannot intrude on nature, you see, and build your screen, because it would not be natural, and you know Kruger must always remain natural."

"But Albert," she says, gesturing to the dining area, "you can't say *this* is natural."

Machaba follows her gaze and gives a little yelp of amusement.

No one could help but smile at the scene. An American—me—was finishing his hamburger. With each bite I took, more birds from the bush fluttered in and landed on my picnic table, anticipating the crumbs I would leave. Or I might, as tourists almost always do, toss bread from the bun to the birds from the bush.

First three, then five, then fifteen, then more than thirty birds pranced about on the table or the nearby chairs or on the rafters of the snack bar shelter. Some were bright metallic, beautiful blue starlings. Others horn-billed with no neck and still others wrenlike and with delicate strutting of wing and leg. Their heads, beaks, and bright eyes bobbed with the motion of the hamburger from hand to mouth to plate and back, some just inches from me. A German family two tables over laugh in delight at the show, and the father of the family reaches for the words in English.

"Al-frrred Hitchhhhh-cock!" he says as even more birds land. "Alfred Hitchcock! *The Birds*."

I lob part of the bun a few feet away. The flock follows it, swirling about like raptors struggling for a spot at the kill.

"No, no, no, I do not think that is natural at all," Albert Machaba says. The woman points, too, to the white splotches of bird poop on the ground, chairs, and tables. "Ohhh!" Machaba says and winces. "No, no, no, I agree that is no good. Let me think. "We must do something, find some balance. Let me think."

For the time being, I am parked with park officialdom, and I plan to spend some hours with Machaba as he goes about his daily routine.

The little problem with the birds was not lost on Machaba. He knew they were a metaphor for larger problems in the park. They had become habituated to humans, and in fact had worked humans into their daily routine. This was easy food with no risk. Of course the birds would keep coming. It was only natural.

And there was the rub. What *was* nature? What *was* natural? Kruger National Park was founded on the principle that nature should remain natural as much as possible. Yet huge as it was, Kruger was not a complete ecosystem. Kruger was not in a pure sense "natural." Fences blocked the western migration of animals to water in the dry season, so wells had been dug and then pumped by windmills to make up for the intrusion of the fence.

More obviously, humans intruded when they viewed nature—and this viewing was a purpose of the park, as well as preservation. It did not matter that there were Do Not Feed the Birds signs plastered all over the dining area. The birds found a way. The tourists obliged the birds. The presence of humans changed things.

Machaba's job was to keep the balance tilted toward nature as much as possible. His area of the park, Satara, was noted in particular for the large size of its prides. Sometimes, in fact, they called Satara the cat camp because there were so many lions. For the most part, the lions lived in large prides and were tough: they specialized, most of them, in buffalo.

Such was the complicated context—the question of what was nature—in which Albert Machaba considered the smaller complexities of his everyday life. It was too intricate a puzzle some days. He welcomed the new authority and the new responsibility. But he missed the old days when he was less of a manager and more of a ranger.

There was nothing sweeter to Albert Machaba than spending the night in the bush. He treasured it. It balanced him. At night he could hear the lions roar, and he would take strength from that, not fear. Long ago, his relatives, men and women of the Shangan tribe, had lived in the park, heard the same roars, and felt the same closeness to the sky and to the land and to Africa.

Long ago, the South African government ordered all the people out of the park. Some of Albert's forebears went west to Jonni. Others of the tribe went east to Mozambique. They were distant from him now, and he did not know their names. He did know that they would always cross the park, if for no other reason than to reunite families and shore up relations within clans and tribes. He knew that some of these refugees crossing the park must in some way be his distant relatives and kinsmen. In the bush, alone, under the stars, he could see how these movements were natural and would continue.

But the cell phones, the beepers, the radios, the walkie-talkies, the seemingly unsolvable little problems like the birds—those things bothered him endlessly. He had little time. He had little peace. He sometimes worked seven days a week, sometimes with little sleep.

A bridge needed repair. A car had broken down. A brush fire. Always, they were fighting brush fires. More and more there were brush fires. The refugees set them, he knew, to scare away the lions and to keep warm.

Tourists would call in to report an emergency. A wild dog seemed to have a broken leg. The tourists were concerned and wanted Albert to patch up its leg. Yet, how was he to help the wild dog if the balance of nature was to rule in Kruger? Then again, how was he to tell a family with children of eight, ten, and twelve years old that it was best that the wild dog with the broken leg fend for itself? That it was, after all, the way of nature for the weak to feed the strong?

How did you resolve problems like this one: in 1998 three Mozambican brothers were attacked in the park. Two came to Machaba and begged him to help the third brother; they could not drive the lioness off. Several rangers assembled, and at several hundred meters Machaba could see that the lioness was on top of the man.

So with a backup of rangers with lesser rifles, Machaba sighted down the scope of his .458 magnum, enough gun to bring down an elephant. There was no sport here. Heart shots and head shots were the two choices, and Albert put the crosshairs on the head. He squeezed, the big gun bucked, and what was left of the lion's head jerked and fell limply across the Mozambican, who was already dead and partly eaten.

"It was a sad day," Machaba said. "Sad for the man. Sad for the lion. But when we catch them red-handed, we must kill them. There is no looking away from that. We cannot look away then, no."

But it was hard. All of these conflicts and duties rained down on him.

Still, some days were as simple and straightforward as the most basic rules of the park. Humans stayed in the cars. No exceptions. They were to be back in the camps by nightfall, no options. The camps were actually low-security forts, with motel-like huts and concessions behind barbed-wire fences, with guards at the entry points.

Humans could be foolish, of course, and as I was making rounds with Machaba one day, he spotted an expensive E-class Mercedes pulled over away from the road, partly hidden by trees.

An older man was at the wheel and the passenger-side door was open. Machaba could see, through his glasses, a white woman on the other side of the Mercedes, squatting, panties round her ankles, emptying her bladder. Both were Afrikaners and of the age that helped bring on the laws of apartheid. No doubt they benefited from those oppressive rules.

There were many ways a ranger might approach such an incident. The first would be official and by the book. The second would be cruel and revengeful, extracting humiliation for the decades of discrimination. A third was Machaba's way.

"She is making her water," Machaba said to me. "I will give her a moment."

He looked away and waited with respect until the woman was done and back in the car. Then he approached with ticket book in hand.

"Hello, hello, hello," he sang out in a friendly tone, but with his ticket book plainly in sight. "Sir, madam, good day to you.

"So I understand what you have done here, yes," he said, "and this time I will not give you a ticket for this mistake. But sir, madam, you must please listen. What you are doing is very dangerous. You must listen.

"You see, you have pulled off the road and into the bush, thinking to hide and have some privacy, or perhaps it is cooler here, or perhaps you are hiding from those nasty rangers. Yes, those nasty rangers.

"But this is the same thought that the lions have, you see, and they often in the daytime lay up in thickets *exactly* like this."

He pointed to the tangle of vegetation and trees that the woman had just watered.

"So then what might happen, you see, is the lion jumps out and hurts you and maybe even kills you and then do you know what happens? What might happen that is even worse than that?" Machaba asked in deadpan.

"Well, it is simple: if you are eaten, I will get in trouble," he said. "And so will the lions. You can see how this is not good."

The man and woman got the small joke and smiled with understanding—and appreciation that they had escaped a ticket.

"Next time," Machaba said. "If you are eaten? I will have to give you a ticket."

The couple started the engine and drove away, waving back to him with smiles.

"Please, please, stay on the road and do not be eaten," Machaba said softly to himself.

The joke, he knows, is a darker one than any tourist may ever know. Always, it keeps popping up. Often, in the course of their patrols, Machaba and his rangers come upon tattered bits of clothing. A wallet with Mozambique currency. A full water bottle. Machaba was used to the rationalizations, and perhaps he had used them himself once or twice.

"No, no, no, no," Machaba will say when asked about these things now. His voice is mellow at such times, but with a sad, resigned undertone.

"I do not think that people with nothing would leave one shoe. I do not think refugees with no clothes would leave a suitcase with clothes behind. I do not think that poor people would throw away their wallets. I do not think that is what is happening at all."

Like the birds in the dining area, Machaba knows, lions in the park have become too accustomed to humans. Like the birds in the dining area, they have found an easy source of food. Unlike the birds in the dining area, some lions do not wait for the humans to provide them crumbs. And unlike his conflict and confusion over the bird problem, Machaba has had time—years, actually—to consider the lion problem. And he believes he knows what can solve it.

After all was said and done, the conventional means had been tried and proven unworthy. In the Beowulf legend it was the same. No sword or arrow could pierce Grendel's hard skin, no spear could harm him. Only when Beowulf closed with Grendel in hand-to-claw combat did the hero win by ripping from the monster's shoulder socket the entire arm of the beast.

Albert Machaba, too, was done with conventional wisdom and techniques. On a crisp, cold, sunny morning in July 2000, he drove from left to right on the map, heading from west to east, from Kruger toward Mozambique.

This was the advantage of being in charge of the Satara district. He got to enforce rules. And in the best tradition of Stevenson-Hamilton, park founder, lion savior, Machaba also got to break, or maybe just bend, the rules a bit.

So Albert steered his four-wheel-drive truck east toward Mozambique. It was a forty-five-minute drive to the border road and the fence that sealed it. A half hour of that drive was past parched lands where Kruger had burned. Was burning. You could see the low fires creeping forward through the grass. The rangers could not contain them all. Tourists asked more and more about the fires, and the rangers stumbled over how to explain them all.

He reached the border road and drove another ten minutes north in South Africa and then reached a special padlocked gate. Albert jumped out and undid the padlock, swung the gate wide, drove his truck through the opening, got out, closed the gate, and drove on.

There were no border guards, though the Mozambicans knew he was coming. There were no passport checks. Though his superiors were aware of this trip, they were not *officially* aware. No record would be kept of his travel and therefore no official sanction to singe his superiors if Machaba's gambit blew up.

He drove east on a lonely road. The trees, the land, the soil itself seemed spent. There were no animals and few birds. People he passed looked at him oddly—a well-nourished, well-dressed black man in a white man's truck. He would occasionally see the flag of Mozambique Some flags contain the tools of a nation that are typical of its industry or people. Mozambique is no exception. The AK-47 rifle image still waves from its flag in peacetime.

Soon, Albert came to a village with the equivalent of a county hall, and there he met some men who wore uniforms similar to his, though they bore the colors of Mozambique, not South Africa, and were clearly not as new or clean as Albert's. The men talked, and it was clear Albert had been expected.

They passed some time in small talk, and then Albert began.

"Listen, I must tell you about the park," he said. "I know that your people and your relatives or your friends or your cousins will cross. I know you will always cross, I know you have to cross. I understand these things.

"These are the things you must do, please. You must not be eaten by lions! Do you know why? This is important. Because if lions eat you, then the newspapers will write about you being eaten and they will make trouble for me. You will please, please do me this favor and not be eaten, so I stay out of trouble and so the lions stay out of trouble. This is so because we need the lions. We need the lions so the tourists will come. We need their money so all of us get better and earn money for our families."

Then Albert Machaba told them what they must do. They must travel in groups of thirty. They must hire a guide.

"And if you travel in groups of thirty with guides, you will be safe, or as safe as you can be," Machaba continued. "You will be able to scare away the lions if you stay together."

Then he told them the truly controversial part.

"*If* you cross in groups of thirty, if you are not eaten by lions? I will not stop you or try to catch you. I have much better things to do. And I know you will keep coming even if I try to catch you. You must keep coming, to see your people, your families, to find jobs and send the money back. You must eat.

"Also, though, you must not set fires at night! The fires hurt the park. The fires get me in trouble, too, and you must not set fires. If you set fires, then I will come and have to catch you. But if you do not set fires? I will not chase you. I will let you pass. Even if I see you. Do you all understand?"

They nodded their heads yes. Yes, they understood this black man who talked their language and understood the park. Yes, they would follow his advice. And they would spread the word, too.

"Tell everyone," Machaba said. "Tell them all what I have said here today."

"Please do not be eaten and get me in trouble," he would say a hundred times. And the little joke would travel to three hundred more people through those he had told.

He did not stay long at this village. He drove farther east to the next village. He gave the speech. Then headed north to another village and gave the speech. Then east again for another speech. He stayed the night and then was up again, talking to government officials. The message was always the same. You have a free pass going west to Jonni. Travel in large groups. Use a guide. No fires. Do that and he, the district manager for the whole large central region of Satara, a full one-third of the park, said that you did not need to worry about the rangers. In effect, the social advantages of human beings were restored. The natural tendency of prey species to group together for protection was encouraged. The more people, the more likely predators will be detected.[144] This ancient defense against predators was endorsed. Just as important, the other predators of the refugees, the park rangers, would not apprehend them.

That was in July 2000. Nothing happened right away. In fact, nothing happened at all for the rest of 2000, the rest of 2001, the rest of 2002, and the rest of 2003. No reports came of lion kills of refugees in 2004 or 2005 either.[145]

Nothing was good.

"I think you may have something here," Gertenbach said to Albert finally, and so it seemed. Machaba makes the trips still to this day, every month for two days, telling Mozambicans clearly they all can come if they are careful.

Machaba, it seemed, had found his balance. The monster he killed was not a lion but the system that assured a conveyor belt of easy human prey. Curiously, Machaba's solution was not tried elsewhere in the park. The official explanation of why not is perhaps revealing of a casual attitude still toward the deaths of refugees: Machaba never suggested trying it elsewhere, perhaps because it was an "off the record" op.

In the Po-Mo world, at least in Africa, the Beowulf myth of confronting the monster no longer plays well, if ever it did. The functional myth and legend that works is more akin to the trickster stories of Africa—transported to America as Br'er Rabbit. Albert—and Stevenson-Hamilton, too, a century earlier—slyly broke all the bad rules for all the best reasons. And in this one section of the park, it seems, our species has adapted and socially evolved. The Machaba method seemed to work well. For several years, there have been no reported killings—though kills continue elsewhere.

The rest of Kruger functioned pretty much the way it always has in recent years. The refugees come at night. As do the lions.

Chapter 12

ONE LAST TRIP

I bid good-bye to Neville and Steve; an encounter with
tourists and lions; the modern muti of the tourist class;
a thing held in common with the lions of Kruger.

The safari has been a success in many ways, but my goal of walking
the park was going nowhere.

Albert says it would be illegal for him to take me. A photographer
friend says I might find a group of refugees in Mozambique ready to
cross, but then what? "My heart goes out to them," he said, "but these
are desperate people. When you are watching for lions, who is watching *your* back? The gear you would carry on a trip like that is the
equivalent of two years' income for a refugee—in good times. The
odds are it would not be the lions who would get you. There are good
people there, but there are desperate people, too, and there are some
who would kill you from behind just for your shoes."

I try lodge owner Paddy Buckmaster and former refugee John
Khoza, but they shake their heads. They too think it foolish. Besides,
it has been so long; John has few contacts in Mozambique now. For
damned sure, he's not going through the park again. Third time is not
a charm in that trek.

Could I persuade Neville? I played around with the rules of
the combat correspondent. The Rules of Maz—my good friend
Tom Masland. Get the story. But find a good fixer. Then listen to

the person you've hired who knows the culture and the dangers. My fixers are Steve and Neville. They used to go swimming with crocs and pythons. And *they* clearly have said no. They take calculated risks in the bush, but not harmful ones. This sort of foolishness is not in their own code of the bush. And I have been around them long enough to understand at least part of that code and to respect it.

For that matter, the sortie did not meet my journalistic code either. And it would not be allowed under the Rules of Maz either. It is important to witness events and conflicts and to get the stories. But did good journalists *create* the conflicts they were involved in? The journalists I admired did not. Tom did not. None of my friends— "journalistos" I call them fondly—contrived their tight squeezes, nor ever have I, and that is how my plan to walk the park began feeling to me. As a contrivance, maybe even an entrapment of the lions. In the States I'd seen enough gas-bag "journalists" on cable networks contrive entrapments galore for politicians. The risk of becoming one of them is one reason I turned down Washington bureau offers years back. If I did not inflict such deeds upon politicians, to paraphrase Steve, "Why would I want to do something like that to a beautiful animal like the lion?"

So I say good-bye to Steve and Neville, both of whom I've grown quite fond of. I wish them both luck, particularly Neville who needs luck. It seems sometimes that with the same fervor the croc hunter has for finding trouble, trouble finds Edwards. Finally, I hear the last of the cobra stories.

Ever helpful, ever buoyantly optimistic, Edwards, while leading a safari of six vehicles in 1998, pulled off the track to help a tourist change a tire. While he was working, a spitting cobra slipped into his Land Rover under the passenger seat. Tire changed, Edwards popped back into his Landie and led the five other vehicles down the road. He looked for his radio microphone, but the damned thing had slipped under the passenger seat, as it always did. He reached down, felt the microphone cord, pulled it up—and found he was holding the tail of a cobra.

The spitting cobra nailed Edwards expertly; only his wraparound Ray-Bans protected him from the venom. Then, peering through sunglasses murky with milky venom, still holding the snake, dodging the spits of venom, Edwards continued driving down the road. The convoy behind him could see the weaving cape of the cobra rise from the seat of the car. Edwards kept yanking the tail to keep the serpent off balance. On one side, the snake dodged and weaved, trying to get a bead on Edwards. On the other side, Edwards dodged and weaved his head, trying to avoid the cobra's projectiles. The vehicle itself was careening about the road. He could not throw the cobra out without risking a bite. And he was too preoccupied with the snake to bring the Landie to a stop.

Short term, Edwards was doing fine, but quickly computing the odds on the future of holding on to the tail of a cobra, he shifted the Landie into its highest gear and then bailed out the door while the vehicle was still traveling thirty kilometers per hour.

He landed safely with a bump and a scratch. The Land Rover turned into the bush, ran one hundred yards, stalled, and stopped. Neville crept up on the vehicle, opened the door as a chauffeur might, and saw the cobra disembark as if headed to the Oscars. The rest of the convoy watched the whole show, and when Edwards drove back to the road, the group gave him a standing ovation.

When Steve hears the story again, he shakes his head ever so slightly, but a smile still twists up his lips. They are joined at the hip, these two opposites, the straight man and the ebullient comedian. And it is hard to say good-bye to them.

Suzanne and I do say good-bye one day in August outside the park. Neville seems happier, more whole, than when we first met. Steve has been negotiating for days now on a 4x4 truck via cell phone and seems to have closed the deal. Both men close out our safari and start their new journeys.

* * *

I'm on my own now, with the thought of finding an ethical way to walk the park still lingering just faintly. So I hire two earnest young Kruger Park rangers to take me for a by-the-books game-walk through Kruger at dawn. Perhaps at dawn the lions still will be there. I am hopeful. It is then that I cross in the predawn darkness of the Satara camp and hear the lions roar off in the distance. I freeze in midstep as the lizard part of my brain locks down motion, and I stay that way before moving on at a measured pace. I feel for that moment what refugees might feel, but that's not enough to accomplish what I want, to come into contact with lions at short distance in the wild. If not at night perhaps I would get some feel of it in the early hours of dawn, before the night predators are completely done with their work.

The rangers are straightforward. They confess early on that they rarely see lions in the daytime, even at dawn. Each of them carries a .375 H&H and I walk between them. The rangers, a young man and a young woman, have never had to fire in the wild. "The lions see us and run," one says. "Well, let's hope for the worst then," I tell them. "First time for everything," and they smile wryly and exchange glances, smart kids puzzling out what sort of client they have this time.

Dawn breaks and it is a nice walk in the woods. The daylight, after all, is still the province of mankind, not lion. The lions know those rules. We see many tracks and scat markings and a lot of animals and birds, but no lions. I fish for more information and say, "I've heard stories that the lions and the refugees don't get along so well here." They don't bite. They just exchange brief glances again, smile at me knowingly and remain silent. I break out a pack of cigarettes—a short-term secret vice I hide from my wife and daughter—and ask if it is OK to smoke. They say yes, of course, everyone in South Africa does. Could they bum one, and was it true you could get arrested for smoking in America?

We talk informally about their future. "We are doing it while we are young," the woman says, exhaling smoke into the sandalwood-scented air, "and because we love it. I do not know if we can do it forever. The pay is poor, and there are no health benefits."

"I am visiting Amsterdam," the young man says. "I will have to make a decision as to whether this is realistic to do. I want it to be, but I am not sure. It may be better in the city."

The rangers are good company and good guides, but by now I have abandoned getting any real sense of what refugees feel in the park. Part of me feels like I've wimped out; another part says I'm just being wise. Regardless, the door is closed.

But of course, as Taoists, philosophers, barflies, bad marriage counselors, and good fortune cookies will tell you: one door closes; another opens.

What none of them adds is that some days it can be a trapdoor you figuratively fall through, and then drop several links down the food chain.

It is completely unexpected and could not be foretold. I sign up for a night drive in Kruger. On a July evening in 2002, I board an open safari vehicle and rumble into the great African night. Suzanne, my wife, is my photographer on this sortie. She has low-light film, strobes, and a bag of cameras and lenses at the ready. We do not expect much. It has the air of a Great Adventure Tour off Exit 6A on the New Jersey Turnpike.

Instructions are brief. Stay inside the open vehicle. Do not break the profile of the truck and show yourself. No noise. Do not talk. There is no warning about trigger points. Talk and the game will run, we are told. We simply drive, and in fact such drives have been safe over the years.

Big, million-candlepower spots, standard equipment on the vehicle, bleach the near roadside in a white light. I'm handed one to deploy. The black of the African night swallows the beams a few feet into the bush, but the lights scour the near terrain, catching the eyes of all the creatures. A set of green eyes. Kudu. A gray rock that moves. Elephant. Yellow eyes. A serval cat. We peer into the bush, looking for the alchemy of lions formed from the grass, just as they were in daytime. But they are not there.

When we do see them, it is not in the bush but the road. In ordered single file, a hunting platoon of eleven lions from a pride of twenty-five move languidly down the road. This is not your daytime lion. This is *Panthera leo* nocturnal. Lithe and powerful, they swagger, all balls and confidence, like an urban youth gang patrolling turf. There is attitude so utter it need not be displayed, save through a bored and lazy look of cool contempt and power. As Camacho said, "At nighttime, they are a completely different animal." And we see that now.

We pull even with them and are among them. Motor drives whir. Camera strobes freeze the cats. They stare at wheel level but ignore us, an arm's length up and out from them.

What happens next I might be seeing through a lens of too much information, too much listening to Gerrie Camacho and his talk of comfort zones and trigger points. Perhaps the stories around the campfire conjure ghosts in the smoke.

Yet it happens. Yet we see what we see and hear what we hear.

The power and the coiled potential for violence begin to undo the crowd. There are lions everywhere, inches away. Human invulnerability is stripped. First, it is a woman in the back. In a tremulous voice, she says in an English South African accent, "Driver! Please. Turn back. I am afraid they will jump in the car!"

An older man joins in. "Yes! Yes! Turn back please!" he barks. "They are too close. Too close. Turn back!"

Then, on the brink of tears, rattled badly by the adults, a young girl of about eight says in the shakiest of voices, "Let's *do* go home. Let's *do* go home. *Please*! I am very afraid. They are going to jump onto us."

There is no response from the driver, but the lioness nearest us twitches, instantly looks up, then turns her head toward the sound of the child. She has been angling toward the vehicle, and perhaps she truly sees it for the first time and this is the cause of her alertness. Or perhaps she has heard the trigger sound of the child. Her face seems both piqued and confused. She looks up, up, and backs away, powerful back legs feeling for footing, coiling under her, it seems, though she might be reacting to the downward slope of the road. A million candlelights shine in her vision. I'm five feet from her, holding the light directly on her eyes, the tourist guy designated to run the spotter light. Brave Suzanne leans over me, even closer to the big cat, and lets pop with strobe and Nikon at a range of about three feet. For whatever reasons, we both are occupied and calm, focused on our tasks.

But from within the bursts of light come the sounds of fear from other tourists; their amygdalae are working just fine. The lioness hears the sounds of weakness. Her hind legs bend more as she backs. Footing? Or a leap? Trigger point? Or ghosts from the campfire?

Schaller, in his book *The Serengeti Lion*, published drawings by Richard Keane that showed the various facial expressions of lions. The most ferocious face—snarling, teeth displayed—often is the least dangerous. The expression is one of ferocity, but also of fear, a warning display. Think full MGM—the roaring, snarling lion of Metro-Goldwyn-Mayer movies. The snarling trademark actually signals as much fear as fierceness. Often, it is shown to copredators—hyenas, leopards, humans.

The true game face of the lion, the time to be fearful of the lion, is when its face seems neutral, when it is focused and intent.

This is the game face it shows to prey. There is no doubt. Camacho's words come back to me: "and you *know* when they look at you when they want you for food."

This is the face. She is searching. The tourists sense it. More of the adults are chorusing now, asking the driver to leave. Some few stalwarts half shout, "No. Stay!" Suzanne speeds to reload. The motor drive signals that the film has rewound, but for some reason it hasn't. She opens the camera, and the bounce-back of my million-candlelight strobe fogs her photos. She curses and changes cameras.

Now nearly all of the tourists are breaking the rules. Talking. Moving. Showing their profiles. Social organization among the homo sapiens is lost. We are a pod of gibbering hominids, soft skinned, with no claws or teeth to speak of, and no tree to climb. The energy in the safari vehicle seems to be building on the fear. Some seemed at the fight/flight mode. And no one was going to choose fight. Flight off the safari vehicle of course would be assuredly futile then fatal.

The girl sniffles and a great bubble of a sob breaks loose and bursts. The lioness again twitches in sharp response and the tourists flinch. Her face is intent, fearless, in full Schaller form. Scanning for the weak sound. The people in the safari vehicle, some of them, now know what the refugees know. They have taken that one-rung step down the food chain into a chilling self-awareness. They perceive themselves for the first time as food, as just another source of Kruger meat. Africa has had its little joke with me. It is not Mozambicans that Africa shows me as prey species, after all. It is us: the affluent white Westerners.

Meanwhile, the lion and I are playing a small game. She angles her head, trying to gain a vantage to squint through the sun in her eyes, to locate what is making the noises of weakness. My job, I figure, is to keep her blind. My light is the defilade. I move the light as she moves, but the safari vehicle is moving slowly and I am losing the direct angle I need.

Soon she will be able to see around the glaring light and into the vehicle. Some part of me thinks that if she jumps my way, I'll smash the light into her face and the electrical shock might jolt her away from us. Not likely. About as useful, say, as Harry Wolhuter's thought to sock his lion in the nose. Oddly, I do not seem worried. Instead, I remain engaged and very present—not what I would describe as brave, just occupied and taking mental notes. It is after all what we came for, the unearned gift that Africa has bestowed. For some reason, the amydgala does not grab control this time. Some others seem in that mode as well, but most are on or beyond the verge of panic. There are more calls to turn back, more sounds of weakness that the cat notes and scans.

Some seem as if they will actually do it, jump the far side of the safari vehicle, and that will go very badly of course.

Then comes a voice of utter confidence, distinctly English in accent and maternal in tone, as brave in its spirit as Johanna Nkuna, the refugee mother.

"There, *there*," the mother of the child says. "They're *just* as scared of you as you are of *them*, my dear! There is nothing to worry about! They are *just* as scared of you."

She coos the mantra to her child and rocks her, coos again about the lion's fear.

There is absolutely no indication that this is true. The lioness is stone-faced and stalwart, still interested, rippled with coils of muscle. But the voice from the bus seems eternally invulnerable, and it has calmed us all, given us this conceit of humans, that the big puddy tat is scared. It has comforted the crowd and perhaps confused the lion. The driver picks up speed from a crawl to a creep. The lioness backpedals, still searching, but backpedaling clearly now, down the slope of the road shoulder as I lose her with my light.

There is an embarrassed silence in the safari vehicle, and a few seconds later it is as if the panicky scene never played, as if some people did not for a few brief moments feel like prey. Yes, we were always safe. We all ascend with confidence back to the top of the food chain and accept the useful myth of our species that, yes, they were just as scared as we were. Yes, the lions were scared of us. Never were we just meat.

It is our *muti*, this belief. It is our magical hyena tail. We have the slightly unsettled stomachs that come from good roller coasters. Phew. Scared there for a moment, but of course it was safe all along.

The lions troop down the road again in single file, for all the world like jocks taking the field, helmets in hand, walking slowly on the sidelines before the game begins.

And then, at another point, the lions do something I recognize at the most basic level. It is familiar and eerily ordered. I cannot put words to it at first. It is that phenomenon again. Looking at the fire, looking at the lions, searching for the words that almost but never quite come.

Then I know instantly what they are doing, for I have done it myself. In the Midwest, in my small farm town, when I still hunted as we all did back then, we would as kids go out in a pack to shoot pheasants, proud of our new ability to drive cars, proud we were trusted with shotguns. We would find a field of standing corn, walk with the cocksureness of youth single file down one side, space ourselves, and then at a signal, at a nod, enter the corn, hunters all in the ancient driving of game before us.

And this now the lions do. In near exact replica of my old primate friends and me. They move to the bush near the road, still in single file, and at some silent signal space themselves. Some look to their left and right, to gauge the span, or double time on the trot to spread out.

Spaced in this manner, when they are comfortable with the intervals, when they are spread out to cover it all and have exchanged many glances, at some other silent signal it seems, they move as one, entering the bush at a studied lope.

They are on the hunt now, the ancient driving of game begun. And they are gone, moving away from us now and our complexities of myths and thought, our hard-shelled, smelly Land Rovers, and our lost memory that we too are mammals who are also still very much a prey species. The lions of Satara are looking for easy prey now, on the hunt, merciless, as they should be, moving east toward Mozambique, as we head west of Eden, back now toward home.

EPILOGUE

The on-the-ground phase of my investigative safari ended in August 2002 and became a paper chase through books and scientific journals. Unfortunately for Mozambicans, killings in or near the park continued. In March 2003, in Phalaborwa, a South African town just a mile outside Kruger, under a sign that read Tourist Gateway to the Grand Kruger National Park, a male lion sauntered down the paved main street at noontime with a dead Mozambican refugee in its mouth. The local police fired shots, and the lion dropped the body but was not killed. It took them three days to find and decide to kill the lion. A man's shirt was in its stomach.[146]

In 2004, a leopard attacked the driver of a night safari and then was struck by a car. Machaba tracked the wounded leopard, saw it was a hopeless case with terrible wounds, and killed it. There was an uproar throughout the country. He had acted too quickly. He was trigger happy. Who hit the leopard with the car? Would the driver be brought to justice?[147]

"The shot heard round the country has quieted now," Albert said some months later.[148] "It hurts us to have to kill animals, but sometimes it is unavoidable."

Suzanne and Sarah returned from Africa a week after my departure, Suzanne with pictures used in a national magazine article and Sarah with a game ranger certificate that showed among other things that she had qualified on a .375 H&H—quite a bit more gun than ever I have shouldered or intend to.

Steve and Neville kept up their Butch and Sundance friendship. Steve and Sharon's business, Esseness Safaris, continued to flourish. Neville was still away from the bush in 2005 but well settled in his role as director of one of South Africa's largest Zulu cultural centers. They see each other often, and have taken Steve's sons to the snake displays just as Steve's father had taken them for a night walk years ago to show them the cobras of the night. Neville has had an ongoing relationship with a woman named Linda for two years now, and get-togethers of the foursome—Neville and Linda, Steve and Sharon—are common.

John Khoza is still prospering in Marloth Park, though his beautiful daughter, Coley, died suddenly in 2004. There was a theory among some of her friends that she actually had been poisoned. She was beautiful. She wore nice clothes. She had a great job. People were jealous. People die for less in Africa, but there was no proof for that theory. Hepatitis was listed as the official cause. Even then, it is hard to understand how easily life can be cut so short so quickly. It is hard to understand how John so desperately dodged lions and rangers and starvation and worked so hard to give his family advantages over those who stayed in Mozambique only to see his child, thriving in first world conditions, take sick suddenly, then die in only four days.[149]

Tom Masland, my journalist friend and best man, ended twenty-five years as a foreign correspondent virtually untouched and returned to New York City as a senior news editor, to be joined by his family a few months later.

The New Maz Rules were this. He had weekends free for the first time in two decades and time to indulge his talent as a musician. He played jazz saxophone after work and got a gig uptown and a gig downtown. I was able to catch the uptown gig once a while back, but not the night this happened. He left his uptown job at Cleopatra's Needle one evening in October 2005, headed for the late-night downtown performance at Bubbles Lounge, when he was struck by a car on Ninety-fifth Street.

I got to the hospital in time to say good-bye and squeeze his arm—about the only part of his body without a tube or IV or bandage wrap. But he never really regained consciousness and died a short time later. The obituary in *Newsweek* bade him an eloquent farewell under the headline "Jazzman, Journalist, Gentleman." Yet it is hard to understand how the life of a man who lived with extreme danger for so many years can be cut short so quickly and casually on a quiet, rainy night in a first world city. I wish I had been there to help. It would have only involved a bit of crypsis—of freezing—on my part and a tug of just inches on Tom's coat. But the amygdala freezes us at the sight or sound of ancient predators, not modern SUVs, and Tom never much cared for hypotheticals in living his life, and he would not appreciate my wasting words on mighta beens.

As for Gerrie Camacho? In 2003, over the objections of residents, he darted the entire pride that prowled through the Marloth Park community and returned the lions to a large, caged area in Kruger for observation. He felt good about that. Letting the lions free-range through Marloth would only result in more killings of humans and the eventual destruction of the whole pride. They belonged in Kruger where they could be wild. Camacho felt he was making progress.

In 2004 a court ordered Camacho to return the lions to the community. The green residents, the court ruled, had the right to risk having lions in their backyards.[150]

"Gerrie," one of his friends in Marloth said, "this will work. Humans and lions lived in balance for thousands of years with no problems, you must agree that is true."

"Not at night they didn't," was his simple reply. "Never. Not ever."

Eventually, the lions were placed in an enclosed area of Marloth and the lionesses spayed. It was nearly the same to Gerrie as if they had been killed. They were no longer wild lions. They were zoolike animals.[151]

Gertenbach retired from Kruger about the same time that the overall administration of the park passed from conservationists and scientists to businessmen and tourist marketers. He was optimistic that Kruger would stay Kruger. But he was not certain.

As for Kruger? The tourist gambit was working.

"Guess what?" asked a feature in the *New York Times* written by the globe-trotting omnivore R. W. Apple Jr. "Some of South Africa's choicest wines and most satisfying food are served far from the bright lights of Cape Town, right in the midst of the wilderness, along a shimmering stream called the N'wanetsi, where hippopotamuses frolic."[152]

In 2004, near the town of Nelspruit, officials at the regional airport cut the ribbon on a new runway extension that allows 747s to land within a half hour's drive of Kruger. No need to fly to Cape Town or Jo-berg first. Flights from Europe and the Americas can go directly to Kruger.

There has been some progress on the immigration issue—substantial progress, in fact. Amid great fanfare in April 2005, the South African government announced a new policy: Mozambicans could enter the country and were not required to have a visa for visits of thirty days or less.

South African President Thabo Mbeki announced the change in Cape Town. He said the restrictions had been "wrong" and had imposed "intolerable hardship." "It was embarrassing that we required all Mozambicans who want to come to have a visa and we required that they pay for their visa in U.S. dollars," Mbeki said.[153]

"It's an open border now," one conservationist told me. "There are no more problems."

The last of the apartheid-era laws had finally fallen, and this no doubt took pressure off Kruger as a pathway. Moreover, there was hope that Mozambique's economy was kicking into gear. The Mozambican city of Maputo was featured in a *New York Times* travel section and was said to be nearly crime-free at night, unlike many

South African cities. The beautiful coastal regions were being redis-covered by foreigners, and the economy was kicking up. Mozam-bique was the "next cool place." Only the more skeptical South African journalists noted that the open border was less significant for Mozambicans—who came to South Africa anyway—and more sig-nificant for big South African companies that could develop Mozambican wilderness shores and attract large numbers of South Africans across the free border.

Still, Mozambique has a long way to go. Lions reportedly devoured more than twenty people in the north province of Cabo Delgado in 2003. The villagers believed the lions were witches taking the form of lions, and angry relatives of the victims beat to death the twelve peo-ple suspected of practicing witchcraft. No arrests were made.[154]

But even as the country modernizes, there always will be the dan-ger of catastrophe, of flood, and drought in Mozambique.[155] And always there will be the pull of family, of tribal ties.

Toward the end of our summer 2005—winter in Africa—the southern part of Mozambique was again struck by drought. As the world focused on other tragedies in Africa, Mozambicans were starv-ing. Not taking extra time to cross at a border checkpoint, they turned west to Eden for food. The lions were still there, awaiting the migration of prey. Still, detention centers for immigrants in 2005 noted a marked decrease in Mozambicans because of the new visa policy and open border.

But they also pointed to a notable uptick in Zimbabweans as that country's economy continued to implode—under the rule this time of a black racist. There is no open border with Zimbabwe. The coun-try borders South Africa, and the least-guarded access to South Africa is through Kruger.

Bertus Swanvelder, a unit leader at the detention center in Lin-dela outside Johannesburg, says the detainees tell familiar tales of how they crossed the park. Unlike Machaba's Mozambicans, they are new to the game. They seem to come with few guides, in massed numbers, then scatter like impalas when they come upon lions. Very slow, soft, tired impalas.

"Some tell us stories of how they were charged by elephants and attacked by lions as they came across Kruger National Park," he said. "They come in a group of fifty but only fifteen survive. They have amazing stories. It breaks your heart sometimes."[156]

They send the Zimbabweans back by train, but detention officials say many of them jump from the speeding train, and on arriving in Zimbabwe the train is often just half full. The refugees then begin the trek back across the park.

"Yes, they will always cross," Albert Machaba said. "They will always cross Kruger because some of them must. They are not going to just lay down and die. They will always cross."

Another controversy stirred in Kruger in late 2005. The black rhinoceros, once near extinction, was present in such numbers within the park that the rangers were thinking of killing five of the oldest. The rhinos seemed to be destroying terrain and plants needed by other species. A trial balloon was floated: charge Western trophy hunters $200,000 to hunt and kill the old rhinos. That would give the park a cool million to help preserve the park.

"The general feeling is that we have a problem and that problem isn't going to go away," said Kevin Rodgers, a professor of ecology at the University of the Witwatersrand in Johannesburg. He is also heading a scientific review of the impact of elephants. Their park population has increased to twelve thousand from eight thousand in 1994, the year culling was stopped.

"Eventually, we're going to have to make hard decisions," he said. Too many elephants in Kruger National Park can threaten eagles. Elephants often knock down the trees they nest in. The herds can wipe out food needed by other species and girdle trees as well. And a too-large population of male rhinos can result in fatal fights. Thus population growth is decreased by distorting the balance between males and females.

The debate is gamely joined, of course, by preservationists—the philosophical descendents of John Muir. And of course, they have some very good points. If animals like the black rhino remain endangered across Africa, then excess animals can be moved to other parks with smaller populations.

There are only an estimated 3,610 black rhinos in the world, for example, and according to the International Rhino Foundation, the populations declined 92 percent between 1970 and 1992.[157]

Jason Bell of the International Fund for Animal Welfare (IFAW) argues that the idea that nature conservation should be linked to economics places conservation on a slippery slope. "I think there's a very strong movement worldwide which is trying to promote the use of wildlife and natural resources, sometimes to the detriment of species," he told the *Christian Science Monitor*. "What we're seeing in Southern Africa is the view that natural resources need to have an economic value to have a place in our world."[158]

The problem with that approach, said Rudi van Aarde, director of the Conservation Ecology Research Unit at the University of Pretoria, is that South Africa's parks become less natural and become more artificial spaces.

He points to East Africa as a superior model. There animals are allowed to roam freely. They move past the boundaries of parks. Kruger is more a conservation fortress. Its fences and wells frustrate normal migration patterns, and natural balances of animals as well. Van Aarde and groups like IFAW have a vision of unfenced conservation areas, all interconnected. These more natural ecosystems would allow elephants and rhinos to die naturally. Normal drought cycles would assure normal balances of animals. Native Africans can share in revenues created through responsible tourism.

"What's the benefit of this? We'll have large conservation areas instead of small conservation areas. We'll have natural limitation of numbers rather than unnatural limitation. We'll have cost-effective conservation instead of costly conservation," van Aarde said.[159]

* * *

There are holes in both approaches. The hunting revenues theory has its attraction and a number of conservationists feel the decline in lion populations paralleled the banning of lion hunts. Ethical hunters truly are committed to maintaining the land in a natural state and their willingness to pay very high fees gives the lion an economic reason for being.

Here's the rub. Not everyone is ethical. As Tom Masland wrote, there are hunters and there are hunters. The statistics released by a recent South African government panel were devastating. More than sixty-seven hundred "hunters" had killed fifty-four thousand animals in game parks outside Kruger. About one hundred ninety lions were killed bringing in $3.3 million, or around $18,000 per lion. The list of animals killed included baboons, giraffes, elephants, hippos, mongooses, porcupines, warthogs, zebras, kudu, and leopards.

South African environment minister Mathinus van Schalkwyk noted that hunting is and should remain an integral part of South African life and some of those animals were killed in fair-pursuit circumstances.[160]

But the canned hunts had shamed the country, he said. Rhinoceroses were hunted with bow and arrow, causing slow, agonizing deaths. Some zebras were crossbred with donkeys to slow their gait and make them slower and easier to kill.

"This is something that no civilized country can continue to tolerate," van Schalkwyk concluded.

All of which makes those black rhino hunts seem a little less attractive a revenue source to me. Van Schalkwyk has proposed legislation to straighten up the hunting scene in South Africa, but his report is a reminder that noble ideas—hunting revenue underwriting conservation—can be corrupted.

The preservationist approach, though, has its own Achilles' heel. To its credit, the movement does not ignore the indigenous and treat them as intruders on nature. Preservationists now often seek to make preservation attractive by sharing low-pressure tourism revenues with local residents. In many cases that works well. It's smart to link the two interests. But in East Africa, there are those who feel the preservationists often lose sight of the fact that the preserved wildlife eats the local residents all too regularly.

One conservationist in East Africa has seen how that works in the case of lions. In August 2005, Craig Packer, the world-respected lion man, published a paper that noted an increase in man-eating behavior in Tanzania.[161] It seemed to me a jolt to the conservationist community and a brave bit of research by Packer that pushes a new paradigm a bit further still.

In a nutshell, he found this: as humans took over more terrain, the lions' regular prey of antelope, wildebeests, and zebras had disappeared.

So the lions shifted to eating bush pigs. Bush pigs raid farmers' crops. The farmers camp out in their fields to defend them from the bush pigs. The lions who chase bush pigs find humans instead.

More than 560 humans have been killed, and 308 have been injured since 1990—far more than in Tsavo so many years ago. The opportunistic seizing of a human after missing a pig appears to have broadened to the hunting of humans in general. The lions are killing people three times as often as fifteen years ago, Packer said, and efforts by conservationists to preserve lions is directly resulting in the loss of human life.

The article in *Nature* got little press play—just a few paragraphs on the wires and a mention in the *Times*.[162] The big story in that edition of Nature was another proposal to "re-wild" the United States West with elephants and cheetahs—animals that lived in North America during the Pleistocene. The elephants, it was suggested, would take care of the growing problem of mesquite spreading all over Arizona.

Packer's lonely voice warning about the increase in man-eating essentially went unheard by the world at large. Eventually, he seems to suggest, the apathy surrounding the deaths of humans in the jaws of lions will backfire to the lions' detriment.

In other words, conservation done wrong, that is, in a manner that assures the death of humans, is wrong on ethical and very practical levels. My thoughts are that eventually, humans will take actions to destroy the lions. If it takes a cheap AK-47 to protect one's field from pigs and one's family from lions, then an AK becomes a necessary agricultural tool. Yes, lions are hard to kill by ethical hunters using hunting rifles. But a full clip from an AK on full automatic would do the job even if fired from the hip by a farmer. So would forty cents' worth of poison, or a few cents' worth of wire shaped into a snare.

Beats being ethical and eaten.

It is not good to ignore the facts and trend line of human consumption, Packer argues, and he comes perilously close—admirably, I would say—to unscientific emotion to make sure that readers understand fully the human toll that is taken.

> Lions pull people out of bed, attack nursing mothers, and catch children playing outside. . . . Most rural houses have thatched roofs and many have thatched walls, so lions force their way inside, and toilets are outside.[163]

"Human population growth has led to encroachment into wildlife areas and depletion of natural prey," Packer said. "However, conservation attempts to sustain viable populations of African lions, place the lives and livelihoods of rural people at risk in one of the poorest nations.

"Mitigation of this fundamental conflict must be a priority for any lion conservation strategy in Africa," Packer concluded.

"A lot of people . . . think predators are cute and cuddly," Packer later told a reporter for the *New York Times*.

"They're not."[164]

As if to prove the point back in Kruger, there were fresh press reports of a new killing in 2005 on the park side of the Phalaborwa gate in the northern area of the park. On August 4, rangers came upon two lions feeding on the corpse of a man. They killed one lion, but the other escaped. A hunt for it was called off after a week, when trackers lost the spoor.

"It will be almost impossible to identify the lion that killed the man at this stage," said William Mabasa, Kruger's head of communications.[165] But the converse of that was also true, of course. By this time, it was nearly impossible to prove that any of the lions could not have done the deed.

The latest killing left the authorities with a public problem. They really did not need yet another dead Mozambican after the open-border rule. At first, they were not sure who the victim was.

"All that's left of him is his skull, a few ribs and the lower half of his body," said Inspector Chris Nel of the Phalaborwa Police Station.[166]

But then a South African family identified the body as that of Thomas Ngobeni, a beloved but sometimes bewildered village resident who would wander into the park. The family recognized his legs and pants and claimed the body, then held an elaborate South African funeral ceremony.

The day after the burial, a social worker arrived to inform them that Thomas Ngobeni was alive, in a hospital, and very much wanted to see them.

"We all became disorientated, especially our mother, who started crying hysterically," said Ngobeni's sister, Christine Ngobeni. "We believed Thomas was already buried in his grave."

The family traveled in a convoy of taxis for one hundred fifty kilometers to Letaba hospital and found Thomas in good physical health. His mother collapsed, and nurses had to revive her.

As it turned out, the police had taken Thomas to the hospital because he was acting "out of his head," a condition the family confirmed was not uncommon. But the family was not notified. They connected his absence with the announcement of the recovered corpse in Kruger and made a logical but errant conclusion.[167]

The question now was who *did* the family bury? The speculation was that it was a Mozambique refugee. Most likely, he will never be identified.

So now park spokesman William Mabasa, a straightforward and well-meaning man, who earnestly has attempted to answer all my questions, once again was stuck with the job of explaining the unexplainable. Only this time, in public statements, he went beyond anything I had heard previously from the park.

"It is natural for lions to keep away from humans. But, they're creatures of habit—if they find it easier to hunt humans, they will continue to do so," he said.

"Humans are easy to hunt and thus become the preferred choice of prey," he added.[168] This was the first official admission I had heard that a number of the lions of Kruger have specialized in humans and are true man-eaters.

He also reminded everyone that there is a 1,500 rand fine (about $250) for entering the park illegally. But there are no other policies under way to combat the problem. Albert Machaba's methods have not been adopted parkwide.

The confusion about the bodies and the mixup of the elaborate funeral—and also the funeral ceremony for my friend Tom Masland—prompted one last question from me to Mr. Mabasa and the park.

What has been done with the remains of the refugees that have been found in the park over the years?

Is there a pauper's field, a cemetery for the unknown refugees? Are the remains kept for scientific study? What happens to the remains? Are they simply disposed of? Cremated?

What is the park policy? Any ceremony at all? Words said? Custom observed? Scripture read? *Muti* bought? Then offered? How does it work? Is there any simple commemoration that a human being once lived?

When I mention the bodies, the park officials for the first time do not reply to a question. And it makes me wonder. If good, truly brave men like Edwards and Camacho instinctively flee the horrid scenes of lion kills, is there that same social instinct for good institutions? Is there something shared, in our amygdala or elsewhere, that repels us from such realities?

And if good men like Edwards and Camacho and Albert Machaba can overcome their instincts to flee and then return to the scene and examine the realities and options, what does it take for good institutions and the rest of us to do the same?

ACKNOWLEDGMENTS

This book would not have been conceived of were it not for friends and family who insisted I visit Africa even though I had just started a new job a few months earlier. Suzanne, my wife, was chief among those as was my daughter, Sarah. John Penek and his family in the States plus Tom Masland and his family in South Africa—Gina, James, Robert, and Richard—also urged me to come. The editors at *Men's Journal*—Sid Evans and David Willey—helped make my second trip possible by commissioning an article on Kruger and the lions in 2002.

My thanks go out as well, of course, to Steve and Neville, who were ever helpful and patient with my questions and quirks, and to Sharon Gibson, Steve's wife, who helped immensely in confirming details of the adventures of Steve and Neville. Should anyone want to see anything in southern Africa, I highly recommend Esseness Safaris as well as the Buckmasters' lodge in Marloth Park.

Gerrie Camacho, John Khoza, and Paddy and Pauline Buckmaster all were of great help, as were various unnamed rangers who, while not going on the record, accurately described the situation and steered me in the right direction.

On the scientific side, Nina Stoyan-Rosenzweig helped curb many assumptions in the original draft of this publication, as did Craig Packer and Paul Funston on the narrow scope of "lion metrics" and the estimation of lion kills. (None of the three buy all of my theories, of course, but it is a better book for their straightforward criticism and disagreement.)

Editor Bill Eddins, whom I have worked with now for more than twenty-five years, tightened the structure of the story and helped ground my writing as only a gifted master carpenter of words can. Christine Duffy, my editor at The Lyons Press, also provided important critiques and encouragement and in fact made this book possible. Sterling Lord, my literary agent, told me how the book could be structured circa 2002; I heard him, finally, circa 2004, and am resolved to listen more quickly next time.

Jane Carruthers and her book about Kruger and her biography of James Stevenson-Hamilton were invaluable to my understanding the park of yesterday and of today.

Albert Machaba, Willliam Masaba, Willelm Gertenbach, and the other park officials were more helpful than I had thought possible. They gave honest and straightforward answers to my questions, which, in this day of "spin" and "staying on message," was as refreshing as it was helpful. It is with that open attitude that one day they may find the solution to the man-eaters of Eden.

Tom Masland was of great help to me in puzzling out what I should and should not do concerning the park crossing. His great spirit and the manner in which he lived his life continue to be a great inspiration to me and he is missed beyond what words can convey.

Finally, I would encourage anyone reading this book who feels the urge to visit Kruger National Park and its environs to act on that urge. The park is both affordable and safe, if one minds the rules of the park and the rules of nature.

BIBLIOGRAPHY

Azevedo, Mario J. *Tragedy and Triumph: Mozambique Refugees in Southern Africa, 1977–2001.* Portsmouth, NH : Heinemann, 2002.

Brennan, Tom. *Refugees from Mozambique: Shattered Land, Fragile Asylum.* Washington, DC: U.S. Committee for Refugees, 1986.

Bulpin, Thomas Victor. *The Hunter Is Death.* Long Beach, CA: Safari Press, 1987.

Capstick, Peter Hathaway. *Death in the Long Grass.* New York: St. Martin's, 1977.

Caputo, Philip. *Ghosts of Tsavo: Stalking the Mystery Lions of East Africa.* Washington, DC: Adventure Press, National Geographic, 2002.

Carruthers, Jane. *The Kruger National Park: A Social and Political History.* Pietermaritzburg, South Africa: University of Natal Press, 1995.

———. *Wildlife & Warfare: The Life of James Stevenson-Hamilton.* Pietermaritzburg, South Africa: University of Natal Press, 2001.

Crush, Jonathon, and Vincent Williams. "Making Up the Numbers." Policy brief no. 3. Kingston, Ontario: Southern African Migration Project, 2001.

Dolan, Chris. "The Changing Status of Mozambicans in South Africa and the Impact of this on Repatriation to and Re-integration in Mozambique." Final Report to the Norwegian Refugee Council, February 1997, http://www.nrc.no/Dokserie/97-2/mozambique.htm.

Du Toit, Johan, Harry Biggs, and Kevin Rogers. *The Kruger Experience: Ecology and Management of Savanna Heterogeneity.* Washington, DC: Island Press, 2003.

Fernandez-Armesto, Felipe. *Millennium: A History of the Last Thousand Years.* New York: Touchstone, 1995.

Grobler, Douw. *African Lion News* 4 (February 2003), www.african-lion.org.

Guggisberg, C. A. W. *Simba.* Philadelphia: Chilton Books, 1963.

Hart, Donna, and Robert W. Sussman. *Man the Hunted: Primates, Predators, and Human Evolution.* Cambridge, MA: Westview, 2005.

Heaney, Seamus, trans. *Beowulf: A New Verse Translation.* New York: Farrar, Straus, and Giroux, 2000.

Herne, Brian. *White Hunters: The Golden Age of African Safaris.* New York: Henry Holt, 1999.

Holgate, Kingsley. *Cape to Cairo: One Family's Adventures along the Waterways of Africa.* Cape Town, South Africa: Struik, 2002

Joseph, Earl, and Dick Parris, eds. *Visions of Change: Social Ecology and South African National Parks.* Pretoria, South Africa: South African National Parks, 2000.

Kerbis-Peterhans, Julian, and Thomas Gnoske. "The Science of 'Man-Eating' among Lions *Panthera leo* with a Reconstruction of the Natural History of the 'Man-Eaters of Tsavo.'" *Journal of East African Natural History* 90, no. 1–2 (2001): 1–40.

Kruger National Park. "Flora and Fauna." Skukuza Camp, South Africa, January 2006, http://kruger-national-park.ask.dyndns.dk/.

Kruuk, Hans. *Hunter and Hunted: Relationships between Carnivores and People*. Cambridge, UK: Cambridge University Press.

Kuipers, Dean. *Ecco-Warrior Groups in the United States*, www.totse.com/en/politics/green_planet/eco-war.html.

Livingstone, David. *Livingstone's Travels and Researches in South Africa*. Philadelphia: J. W. Bradley, 1858.

Packer, Craig, Dennis Ikanda, Bernard Kissui, and Hadas Kushnir. "Lion Attacks on Humans in Tanzania." *Nature* 436 (18 Aug 2005): 927–928.

Patterson, Bruce D. *The Lions of Tsavo: Exploring the Legacy of Africa's Notorious Man-Eaters*. New York: McGraw-Hill, 2004.

Patterson, John Henry. *The Man-Eaters of Tsavo*. Guilford, CT: Lyons Press, 2004. First published 1907 by MacMillan.

Quammen, David. *Monster of God: The Man-Eating Predator in the Jungles of History and the Mind*. New York: Norton, 2003.

Radford, Tim. "Big Dip in Lion Numbers." Manchester (UK) Guardian Newspapers, September 18, 2003.

Roderigues, Jan. *The Game Rangers: 78 Authentic Stories from the African Bush*. Innesdale, South Africa : J. A. Roderigues, 1992.

Ruark, Robert Chester. *Use Enough Gun: On Hunting Big Game*. Long Beach, CA: Safari Press, 1999. First published 1966 by New American Library.

Schaller, George B. *The Serengeti Lion: A Study of Predator-Prey Relations*. Drawings by Richard Keane. Chicago: University of Chicago Press, 1972.

Schmidtz, David, and Elizabeth Willott. "Reinventing the Commons: An African Case Study." Tuscon, AZ, March 3, 2003, http://research.biology.arizona.edu/mosquito/Willott/Pubs/Commons.html.

Seaver, George. *David Livingstone: His Life and Letters*. New York: Harper, 1957.

Smuts, G. L. *Lion.* Johannesburg: Macmillan South Africa, 1982.

Stevenson-Hamilton, James. *South African Eden: From Sabi Game Reserve to Kruger National Park.* London: Cassell and Company, 1937.

Von W. Lambrechts, Arend. "Meeting Wildlife and Human Needs by Establishing Collaborative Nature Reserves: A Transvaal System." In *Integrating People and Wildlife for a Sustainable Future*, edited by John A. Bissonette and Paul R. Krausman, 37–40. Bethesda, MD: Wildlife Society, 1995.

Wolhuter, Harry. *Memories of a Game-Ranger.* Johannesburg: Wild Life Protection Society of South Africa, 1949.

NOTES

1 Brian Keriger and Daniel Fiello, "Daniel Patrick Moynihan—Quotes," Los Angeles, CA, Lexico Publishing Group. http://www.reference.com /browse/wiki/Daniel_Patrick_Moynihan. Author's Note: This seems the most grammatically correct version of the quote, though it often appears as, "Everyone has a right to their own opinion but not a right to their own set of facts."

2 Hart and Sussman, *Man the Hunted*, Page 78. Author's Note: Hart and Sussman in turn reference the twenty-five years of research by New York University Professor Joseph LeDoux.

3 Patterson, Bruce D., *The Lions of Tsavo*, Page 23.

4 Bulpin, *The Hunter Is Death*, Page 305. Author's Note: This a biography of hunter George Rushby.

5 Neville Edwards, interview, Kruger National Park, July 2000.

6 Willelm Gertenbach, interview, Kruger National Park, August 2002.

7 Hart and Sussman, *Man the Hunted*, Page 78.

8 Gerrie Camacho, Mpumalanga Province, July 2002; Livingstone, *Travels and Researches*. Capstick, *Death in the Long Grass*, Page 43. Hart and Sussman, *Man the Hunted*, Page 87. Seaver, *David Livingstone—His Life and Letters*. 1957. New York. Harper and Brothers. Page 79

9 Wolhuter, *Memories of a Game-Ranger*, Page 92.

10 Albert Machaba, interview, Satara Camp, Kruger National Park, August 2002; Douw Grobler, "Lions Change by Darkness." *African Lion News* 4 (February 2003). Page 9–10. http://www.african-lion.org /news4-1part1.pdf

11 Neville Edwards, interview, Kruger National Park, July 2002.

[12] Private game ranger, interview, name withheld, March 2001.

[13] Booker, *The Seven Basic Plots—Why we tell stories*, Page 21.

[14] Fernandez-Armesto, *Millennium*, Pages 445–447.

[15] Caputo, *Ghosts of Tsavo*, Page 4.

[16] Caputo, *Ghosts of Tsavo*, Page 267.

[17] Tim Radford, "Big Dip in Lion Numbers," *Guardian Unlimited*, September 18, 2003, http://www.guardian.co.uk/conservation/story/0,13369,1044522,00.html.

[18] Quammen, *Monster of God*, Page 4.

[19] Hart and Sussman, *Man the Hunted*, Page 33.

[20] Capstick, *Death in the Long Grass*, Page 41.

[21] Capstick, *Death in the Long Grass*." Page 17.

[22] Kruuk, *Hunter and Hunted*, Page 55.

[23] *Stanford Encylopedia of Philosophy*, Chapter Three, "The Paradigm Concept," http://plato.stanford.edu/entries/thomas-kuhn/#3.

[24] Kruuk, *Hunter and Hunted*. Page 55.

[25] From Kruger National Park, Visitors' Map, 1998 statistics; also, Kruger National Park, "Flora and Fauna," http://kruger-national-park.ask.dyndns.dk/.

[26] *Dispatch Online*, "Killer Leopard 'Stressed,'" March 9, 2001, http://www.dispatch.co.za/2001/03/09/southafrica/BLEOPARD.HTM. *Dispatch Online*, "Old, Hungry Leopard Kills Game Ranger," August 25, 1998, http://www.dispatch.co.za/1998/08/25/southafrica/HUNGRY.HTM.

[27] Kruger National Park, "Game Ranger Kills Leopard," press release, May 2003, http://www.sanparks.org/about/media/2003/knp_game_ranger_kills_leopard.pdf; Thandee N'wa Mhangwana, "Three Killed in Kruger Attacks," News 24.com, November 11, 2003, http://www.news24.com/News24/South_Africa/News/0,,2-7-1442_1445497,00.html.

[28] Roderigues, *Game Rangers*, Pages 21–27.

[29] Hart and Sussman, *Man the Hunted*, Page 247.

[30] These accounts are drawn from Wolhuter's *Memories of a Game-Ranger* and from Stevenson-Hamilton's *South African Eden*. The authors differ slightly in their accounts, which were published more than forty years after the incident.

[31] Capstick, *Death in the Long Grass*. Page 42.

32 Wolhuter, *Memories of a Game-Ranger*, Page 313.

33 John Penek, interview, Warren, New Jersey, July 2005.

34 Masland, "Call of the Not-So-Wild" *Newsweek International*, September 2004.

35 Stevenson-Hamilton, *South African Eden*, Page 45. Carruthers, *Wildlife and Warfare*, Pages 82–83.

36 Carruthers, *Wildlife and Warfare*, Page 89, Page 94.

37 Carruthers, *Wildlife and Warfare*, Page 81.

38 Carruthers, *Wildlife and Warfare*, Page 80.

39 Carruthers, *Wildlife and Warfare*, Page 157.

40 Stevenson-Hamilton, *South African Eden, Kruger National Park*, Page 23.

41 Carruthers, *Wildlife and Warfare*, Page 47.

42 Carruthers, *Wildlife and Warfare*, Page 90.

43 Carruthers, *Kruger National Park*, Page 42.

44 Heaney, *Beowulf*, Page 49, Verse 710.

45 Carruthers, *Kruger National Park*, Pages 41–42.

46 Smuts, *Lion*, Pages 175–176.

47 Smuts, *Lion*, Page 173.

48 Smuts, *Lion*, Page 176.

49 Smuts, *Lion*, Page 28, Page 175.

50 Smuts, *Lion*, Page 174.

51 Smuts, *Lion*, Page 173.

52 Carruthers, Kruger National Park, Pages 160–161.

53 Stevenson-Hamilton, *South African Eden*, Page 33.

54 Smuts, *Lion*, Page 178.

55 Gerrie Camacho, interview, Mpumalanga Province, S.A. 2002.

56 Capstick, *Death in the Long Grass*, Pages 15–19.

57 Stevenson-Hamilton, *South African Eden*, Pages 227–228.

58 Stevenson-Hamilton, *South African Eden*, Page 228.

59 Stevenson-Hamilton, *South African Eden*, Pages 227–228.

60 Stevenson-Hamilton, *South African Eden*, Page 234.

61 Carruthers, *Kruger Park*, Page 95.

62 Stevenson-Hamilton, *South African Eden*, Page 236.

63 Schaller, *The Serengeti Lion*, Page 10.

64 Smuts, *Lion*, Page 280.

[65] Smuts, *Lion*, Page 280.

[66] Wolhuter, *Memories of a Game-Ranger*, Page 233.

[67] See Young Peoples Trust for the Environment, http://www.yptenc.org.uk/docs/factsheets/animal_facts/black _mamba.html.

[68] Wolhuter, *Memories of a Game-Ranger*, Page 240.

[69] Holgate, *Cape to Cairo*, excerpt, http://www.exclusivebooks.com /interviews/ftf/kholgate.php?Tag=&CID=.

[70] Azevedo, *Tragedy and Triumph*, Page 139.

[71] Stevenson-Hamilton, *South African Eden*, Page 37.

[72] Albert Machaba, interview, Satara Camp, Kruger National Park, August 2002.

[73] U.S. Committee for Refugees, *Refugees from Mozambique, Shattered Land, Fragile Asylum—An Update, 1988.* Page 12.

[74] South African Migration Project, *Crossing Borders, August 2002*, Page 3.

[75] Boothby, Sulton, Upton. *Children of Mozambique: The Cost of Survival*, Pages 1–3.

[76] Brennan, *Refugees from Mozambique*, 1986, Page 3.

[77] Drumtra. *No Place Like Home: Mozambican Refugees Begin Africa's Largest Repatriation*, Page 9.

[78] Johan Vander Walt, interview, Marloth Park, S.A. July 2002.

[79] Herne, *White Hunters*, Pages 79–93.

[80] Peterhans and Gnoske, *The Science of Man Eating*, Page 10.

[81] Schaller, *Serengeti Lion*, Pages 263–265.

[82] Hart and Sussman, *Man the Hunted*, Page 83.

[83] Private guides, names withheld, interviews, Phinda, S.A., March 2001.

[84] Peterhans and Gnoske, *The Science of Man Eating*, Page 59.

[85] Hart and Sussman, *Man the Hunted*, Page 191.

[86] Gnoske, Peterhans, *The Science of Man Eating*, Page 31.

[87] Harvey and Kat, *Prides—The Lions of Moremi*, Pages 104–105.

[88] Seaver, *David Livingstone—His Life and Letters.* 1957. New York. Harper and Brothers, Page 79.

[89] Capstick, *Death in the Long Grass*, Pages 43–44.

[90] Hart and Sussman, *Man the Hunted*, Page 87.

[91] "Ghosts and Magic in the Kruger National Park," www.vanhunks.com/loweveld1/kruger1.html.

92 "Ghosts and Magic."

93 "Ghosts and Magic."

94 Dolan, *Final Report to Norwegian Refugee Council, Maputo—The Changing Status of Mozambicans in South Africa and the impact of this on repatriation and re-integration in Mozambique.* Chapter IV. "The Loss of a cattle-based economy."

95 *Dispatch Online*, "Kruger Park Lions Hunt Refugees," July 28, 1998, http://www.dispatch.co.za/1998/07/28/southafrica/LIONS.HTM.

96 Azevedo, *Tragedy and Triumph—Mozambique Refugees, 1977–2001*, Page 139.

97 Albert Machaba, interview, Satara Camp, Kruger National Park, August 2002.

98 Mzilikaza Wa Afrika, "Child's Night of Horror Hearing Her Mother Die," *Mail & Guardian*, July 1998.

99 E-mail exchange between the author and Punda-area park police managers.

100 Capstick, *Death in the Long Grass*, Pages 5–6.

101 Joseph and Parris, *Visions of Change*, Page 87.

102 Albert Machaba, interview, Satara Camp, Kruger National Park, August 2002.

103 Joseph and Parris, *Visions of Change*, Page 87.

104 Schmidtz and Willott, "Reinventing the Commons." http://research .biology.arizona.edu/mosquito/Willott/Pubs/Commons.html.

105 Schmidtz and Willott, "Reinventing the Commons." http://research .biology.arizona.edu/mosquito/Willott/Pubs/Commons.html.

106 Big Five Pharmaceutical Company, "The Trend Towards Game Ranching in Southern Africa," 2001 http://bigfive.jl.co.za/profit%20 and%20honour%20in%20game%20ranching.htm.

107 Kuipers, Dean. *Ecco-Warrior Groups in the United States*, http://www.totse.com/en/politics/green_planet/eco-war.html, 1993.

108 Paddy Buckmaster and Gerrie Camacho, interviews, Mpumalanga Province, July 2002.

109 Bulpin, *The Hunter Is Death*, Page 88–89.

110 Big Five Pharmaceutical, "The Trend Towards Game Ranching."

111 Patterson, Bruce D., *The Lions of Tsavo*, Page 28

112 Bulpin, *The Hunter Is Death*, Page 303.

[113] Packer, "Lion Attacks on Humans," also, from author's e-mail exchanges with Packer, 2005.

[114] Gerrie Camacho and Dr. Willelm Gertenbach, e-mail exchanges with author, 2002 and 2003.

[115] Crush and Williams, "Making Up the Numbers." Paragraph 2.2 http://www.queensu.ca/samp/sampresources/samppublications /policybriefs/brief3.pdf.

[116] Willelm Gertenbach, interview, Kruger National Park, August 2002; Crush and Williams, "Making Up the Numbers." Author's Note: Crush and Williams question the army estimates of a 25 percent catch rate, but in the author's opinion, this rough rule appears to correlate with the estimates by immigrations agencies of total Mozambicans crossing the park.

[117] Crush and Williams, "Making Up the Numbers."

[118] Azevedo, *Tragedy and Triumph*, Page 3.

[119] Crush and Williams, "Making Up the Numbers."

[120] Crush and Williams, "Making Up the Numbers."

[121] Stevenson-Hamilton, *South African Eden*; Gerrie Camacho, interview, Mpumalanga Province, July 2002.

[122] Albert Machaba, interview, Satara Camp, S.A. August 2002.

[123] This is the author's conclusion based on interviews and e-mails from various experts, including Craig Packer who believes the projections are faulty and too high, and Gerrie Camacho who believes the projections are too conservative.

[124] Albert Machaba, interview, Satara Camp, S.A. August 2002.

[125] Albert Machaba, interview, Satara Camp, S.A. August 2002.

[126] Grobler, "Lions Change by Darkness." *African Lion News* 4 (February 2003). Page 9–10. http://www.african-lion.org/news4-1part1.pdf. Author's Note: There is some confusion about when the tree incident occurred. In his article, Grobler places the incident in 1992, while both Machaba and Gertenbach placed it in 1997 during interviews. Grobler gives no date for the specific darting he mentions, but his article is dated February 2003. Also see, Chris Erasmus, "Lions Make an Easy Meal of Desperate Refugees," *Herald Sun* (Australia), August 17, 1997, 37.

[127] Patterson, J. H., *The Man-Eaters of Tsavo*, Page 25.

[128] Bulpin, *The Hunter Is Death*, Page 347.

129 Capstick, *Death in the Long Grass*, Page 137.

130 Stevenson-Hamilton, *South African Eden*, Pages 274–275

131 Stevenson-Hamilton, *South African Eden*, Pages 269–271.
Author's Note: The story of Mafuta's death was reconstructed
by trackers for Stevenson-Hamilton.

132 Stevenson-Hamilton, *South African Eden*, Pages 198–199.

133 Stevenson-Hamilton, *South African Eden*, Pages 198–199.

134 Caputo, *Ghosts of Tsavo*, Page 254.

135 Stevenson-Hamilton, *African Eden*, Page 199.

136 Caputo, *Ghosts of Tsavo*, Page 256.

137 Capstick, *Death in the Long Grass*, Page 50.

138 Capstick, *Death in the Long Grass*, Page 50.

139 Herne, *White Hunters*, Page 320.

140 Stevenson-Hamilton, *South African Eden*, Page 198.

141 Capstick, *Death in the Long Grass*. Page 20.

142 Albert Machaba, interview, Satara Camp, Kruger National Park,
July 2002.

143 Smuts, *Lion*, Page 219.

144 Hart and Sussman, *Man the Hunted*, Page 245. Author's Note: The
authors state as survival strategy number one for our ancestors: "Live
in relatively large groups of 25–75 individuals. Safety in numbers; one
of the main reasons all dirurnal primates live in groups is predator
protection. More eyes and ears alert to the presence of predators is the
first line of defense."

145 From a series of interviews and e-mails between Albert Machaba and
author, 2002 through 2005.

146 *Dispatch Online*, "Troops, Police Hunt Man-Eating Lion," March 5,
2002, http://www.dispatch.co.za/2002/03/05/southafrica/blion.html.

147 From an exchange of e-mails with Albert Machaba, 2004.

148 Albert Machaba, e-mail exchange with author. 2004.

149 Paddy Buckmaster, e-mail exchange, September 2005.

150 Wildlife Action Group bulletin, November 27, 2003, Marloth Park;
Gerrie Camacho, e-mail exchange. 2004.

151 Gerrie Camacho, interview, Mpumalanga Province, July 2002.

152 R. W. Apple, "Meals in the Bush, Now with Fine Wines." *New York
Times*, June 22, 2005.

153 "SA, Mozambique, Waive Visas," BuaNews, April 19, 2005,
http://www.southafrica.info/public_services/foreigners/immigration/
moz-130405.htm.

154 "Lions Spark Deadly Witch Hunt," *Mail & Guardian* Online, May 6,
2003, http://www.mg.co.za/articledirect.aspx?area=%2fbreaking
_news%2fbreaking_news__africa&articleid=19740.

155 Xinhua News Agency, "Drought Affects Parts of Center, South
Mozambique," Xinhua News Agency, September 26, 2005.
http://wwwnotes.reliefweb.int/w/rwb.nsf/6686f45896f15dbc852567
ae00530132/f9d83a8fe70d040949257089000e3a98?OpenDocument.

156 South African Migration Project. News. http://www.queensu.ca/samp
/migrationnews/article.php?Mig_News_ID=1812&Mig_News_Issue=9
&Mig_News_Cat=8

157 Itano, Nicole, "Hunt a Rhino, Save an Eco-system?" The *Christian Science
Monitor*, http://www.csmonitor.com/2005/0425/p01s04-woaf.html.

158 Itano, Nicole, "Hunt a Rhino, Save an Eco-system?" The *Christian Science
Monitor*, http://www.csmonitor.com/2005/0425/p01s04-woaf.html.

159 Itano, Nicole, "Hunt a Rhino, Save an Eco-system?" The *Christian Science
Monitor*, http://www.csmonitor.com/2005/0425/p01s04-woaf.html.

160 Groenewald, Yolandi. "Zonkeys and Ligers for Canned Hunts," *Mail &
Guardian* Online, August 31, 2005. http://www.mg.co.za/articlePage
.aspx?articleid=255238&area=/insight/insight__national/.

161 Packer, "Lion Attacks on Humans in Tanzania," *Nature* Volume 436/18
(August 2005): Pages 927–928.

162 Fountain, Henry, "Call of the Wild, or, Rather, the Grim Reaper?" The
New York Times, August 28, 2005. Section Four, Page 3. http://select
.nytimes.com/gst/abstract.html?res=FB0E13FB345A0C7B8EDDA
10894DD404482.

163 Packer, "Lion Attacks on Humans in Tanzania," *Nature* Volume 436/18
(August 2005): Pages 927–928. (Italics mine.)

164 African Eye News Service, "Hunt Called Off for Kruger Park's Man-
Eater Lion," August 4, 2005. http://www.pretorianews.co.za/index
.php?fSectionId=1702&fRequestedUrl=%2Findex.php%3FfSectionId%
3D665%26fArticleId%3D2815953.

165 Fountain, Henry, "Call of the Wild, or, Rather, the Grim Reaper?" *The New York Times*, August 28, 2005. Section Four, Page 3. http://select .nytimes.com/gst/abstract.html?res=FB0E13FB345A0C7B8EDDA1089 4DD404482.

166 African Eye News Service, "Hunt Called Off for Kruger Park's Man-Eater Lion," August 4, 2005. http://www.pretorianews.co.za /index.php?fSectionId=1702&fRequestedUrl=%2Findex.php%3Ff SectionId%3D665%26fArticleId%3D2815953 (Sign on required.)

167 News24.com, "Buried Lion Victim Found Alive," August 25, 2005. http://www.news24.com/News24/South_Africa/News/0,,2-7-1442 _1759874,00.html.

168 African Eye News Service, "Hunt Called Off for Kruger Park's Man-Eater Lion," August 4, 2005. http://www.pretorianews.co.za/index.php ?fSectionId=1702&fRequestedUrl=%2Findex.php%3FfSectionId%3D6 65%26fArticleId%3D2815953 (Sign on required.)

INDEX